BUYING REAL ESTATE IN THE US

The Concise Guide for Canadians

Dale Walters, CPA, PFS, CFP®

Self-Counsel Press
(a division of)
International Self-Counsel Press Ltd.
USA   Canada

Self-Counsel Press acknowledges the financial support of the Government of Canada through the Canada Book Fund (CBF) for our publishing activities.

Printed in Canada.

First edition: 2011; Reprinted: 2012
Second edition: 2016

Library and Archives Canada Cataloguing in Publication

Walters, Dale, 1958-, author

Buying real estate in the US : the concise guide for Canadians / Dale Walters. — 2nd edition.

Includes bibliographical references.

Issued in print and electronic formats.
ISBN 978-1-77040-258-4 (paperback).—ISBN 978-1-77040-766-4 (epub).— ISBN 978-1-77040-767-1 (kindle)

1. House buying—United States. 2. Home ownership—United States. 3. Investments, Canadian—United States. 4. Real estate invest- ment—Taxation—United States. I. Title.

HD255.W35 2015   333.33'830973   C2015-903698-4
                                                C2015-903699-2

Self-Counsel Press
(a division of)
International Self-Counsel Press Ltd.

Bellingham, WA	North Vancouver, BC
USA	Canada

Contents

3 Income Taxes

4 Nonresident US Estate Tax and Probate

5   Other Things You Need to Know   97

Conclusion

Appendix I: Checklist for Buying Real Estate in the US

Appendix II: Resources

About the Author

Figures

Samples

Tables

★ ★

Notice to Readers

Laws are constantly changing. Every effort is made to keep this publication as current as possible. However, the author, the publisher, and the vendor of this book make no representations or warranties regarding the outcome or the use to which the information in this book is put and are not assuming any liability for any claims, losses, or damages arising out of the use of this book. The reader should not rely on the author or the publisher of this book for any professional advice. Please be sure that you have the most recent edition.

Prices, commissions, fees, and other costs mentioned in the text or shown in samples in this book probably do not reflect real costs where you live. Inflation and other factors, including geography, can cause the costs you might encounter to be much higher or even much lower than those we show. The dollar amounts shown are simply intended as representative examples.

Circular 230 Disclaimer: Nothing in this book is to be used or relied upon by anyone for the purposes of avoiding penalties that may be imposed on you under the Internal Revenue Code of 1986, as amended. Any statements contained within this book relating to any federal tax transaction or matter may not be used by any person to support the promotion or marketing to recommend any federal tax transaction. Everyone should seek advice based on his or her particular circumstances from an independent, qualified cross-border tax advisor. No one, without express written permission, may use any part of this book in promoting, marketing, or recommending an arrangement relating to any federal tax matter to anyone else.

★ ★

Acknowledgments

Thos book was seeded during the great recession of 2008, when so many Canadians were buying US properties at bargain basement prices. I began writing the first edition in 2009 and 2010, and it was published in 2011. I mention this because, in an odd sort of way, I have to acknowledge the recession for providing the impetus for me to write this book.

Further inspiration came from my business partner, Robert (Bob) Keats. He was already a successful author when I met him 21 years ago. Bob Keats is the author of a Canadian best-selling book titled *The Border Guide*, now in its eleventh edition, and *A Canadian's Best Tax Haven, The US*, now in its second edition.

Ultimately, if it were not for the support, understanding, and inspiration of my wife, Charlene, and children, Elysha and Neal, I would not have been able to accomplish an undertaking as large as this. Their patience and encouragement allowed me not only to write this book, but co-author a second (*Taxation of Canadians in America*), and a third, (*Taxation of Americans in Canada*).

I want to acknowledge and thank the co-authors of *Taxation of Canadians in America*, Sally Taylor and David Levine, for allowing me the time to update this book while under pressure to complete our next book together, *Taxation of Americans in Canada*.

I also want to acknowledge the KeatsConnelly employees, past and present, for their contributions. They have provided me with knowledge and encouragement at every step along the way.

I want to thank all of the clients I have worked with over the years. It is the clients who have put me in a position to be able to write a book on this topic in the first place; without them it would not have been possible.

Lastly, I want to acknowledge all of the readers of the first edition who provided excellent feedback and were a source for new content ideas.

Introduction

Thanks to the questions and comments I have received since the first edition of the book, I have added new information and clarified existing information. Though much has been added, the book still provides concise information in an easy-to-read format.

Many Canadians have a goal of buying a home in the United States to get some relief from the long and cold winters in Canada. Dreams of days on or near the ocean, or daily rounds of golf in sunny and warm destinations in the US Sunbelt, have inspired Canadians to buy second homes in places like Palm Springs, Phoenix, San Padre Island, and numerous locations throughout Florida.

With record or near-record prices for real estate in Canada, US real estate is a bargain, whether you are simply buying a second home or you are looking to invest in a number of properties. While plenty of opportunity exists, there are several potential pitfalls if you fail to plan or use competent professionals to help you through the process. In many ways, the process seems obvious with few, if any, roadblocks. In fact, it is so easy that many Canadians choose not to seek proper advice, or they get bad advice from people who do not specialize in this area.

An adage I have long lived by is, "just because you can, doesn't mean you should," and that adage is particularly applicable in this situation. On a regular basis I get questions that go along the lines of, "can I do that with the property?" The answer is, nearly always, yes you can do that, BUT you shouldn't. For example, if you asked your realtor whether you can own a property in your corporation, he or she would say yes (which is the correct answer), but would not know to add that you should not own the property in the corporation because it would cause double taxation. If you get nothing else out of this book, I want you to get the fact that you need, first and foremost, to hire knowledgeable professionals to assist you through the process and to change your questions from "can I do this?" to "should I do this?".

While I attempt to answer the most common questions, it is impossible to answer every possible scenario that may arise. Every situation is different; do not rely on the fact that your friend bought a house in a certain way and assume that way will work for you. To begin with, you don't know if your friend received good advice in the first place. Additionally, your facts, circumstances, goals, and timeframes will likely be different from your friend's. I strongly recommend that you seek advice that is customized to your particular situation.

When seeking advice, look for a professional with a substantial amount of cross-border experience. There is a clear pattern that can be seen among the Canadians I talk to; an advisor on one side of the border may give perfectly good advice for one country, but give bad advice overall because he or she did not understand the implications on the other side of the border. It is imperative that your advisor fully understands the implications of any advice on both sides of the border.

I have tried to make a complicated and dry subject readable, and hopefully at least a little interesting, through the use of examples and tables summarizing my points. I have also added notes and cautions throughout to make sure you do not miss important points. Appendix I is a checklist for you to use when buying real estate in the US.

This book is written largely from a tax perspective, so the material can be complex in parts and is forever changing. I hope you agree that this is an essential book for Canadians buying real estate in the US; it is through your comments that I am able to add new material and make improvements. For this reason, I would like it if you would provide reviews of the book on www.self-counsel.com, www.amazon.ca, www.amazon.com, or through whatever site you happened to have purchased the book.

Best of luck in your real estate investing endeavors.

1

Why the US?

When I first wrote this book in 2010, the US real estate market had just crashed, declining up to 70 percent in some areas. The reasons for investing in US real estate were obvious and there were many opportunities for those with the courage and cash to do so. I would guess that the vast majority of those who bought into the US real estate market from 2009–2011 did very well.

Today, opportunities are not as great as they were back then, but millions of US homes continue to be owned by Canadians for many different reasons. Some want to have a second home where the weather is warm; because prices are still a bargain compared to most Canadian markets; because they need to move for work or business; or because they are simply trying out the cross-border lifestyle before making a decision as to whether they will want to spend their winters (or more) in the US upon retirement.

In this chapter I will lay out why buying real estate in the US may still be a good idea for you. I will briefly discuss how short sales and foreclosures work in the US, and talk about currency and why US currency is mostly likely fairly priced; if you are waiting for the US and Canadian dollars to go back to par again, you may be waiting for a long time.

1. US Housing Appears to Be a Bargain

I am not a realtor and cannot give advice on real estate, but as an accountant the numbers are telling me that if I were to purchase and then rent out a US property, I could charge approximately the same amount for rent (after converting for currency differences), but only have to invest about half as much, or less. In essence, I would be doubling my yield, all other things being equal. For example, if I compare Toronto to Fort Lauderdale I find that instead of having to invest, on average, $526,175 USD ($649,599 CAD x $0.81) to receive a gross monthly rent of $2,167 USD, I can invest $171,800 USD, on average, to receive a gross monthly rent of $2,056 USD. The gross annual rent yield in Toronto is 4.94 percent, while the gross annual rent yield in Fort Lauderdale is 14.36 percent.

Table 1
A Comparison of Housing Costs

Market	Home Sale Value	Monthly Cost of Renting[3]
US[1]	$205,670 USD	
Palm Springs, CA	$181,571 USD	$1,800 USD
Phoenix, AZ	$212,087 USD	$1,317 USD
Fort Lauderdale, FL	$171,800 USD	$2,056 USD
Canada[2]	$450,886 CAD	
Montreal	$338,685 CAD	$1,820 CAD
Toronto	$649,599 CAD	$2,675 CAD
Calgary	$465,941 CAD	$2,473 CAD
Vancouver	$905,701 CAD	$2,969 CAD

1 Average price of homes, June 2015, Realtor.com
2 Average price of homes, May 2015, The Canadian Real Estate Association
3 Monthly or renting a three-bedroom apartment, June 2015, Numbeo.com

One of the most important concepts in investing is the fact that diversification reduces risk. Investing in the US provides important diversification that you cannot get by investing in Canada only. Even if you own a number of different types of properties in a number of different locations in Canada, you are still not as well diversified as you could be. The same holds true for your stock or bond portfolio; by holding an all-Canadian portfolio, you have more risk than if you added securities from other countries. Remember that risk is defined as volatility.

US real estate appears to provide more potential upside, better income, and on top of that should serve to reduce the overall volatility (risk) of your real estate portfolio. It appears that all you have to do is to decide if you want one, two, or more US properties.

2. Short Sales and Foreclosures

The words "short sales" and "foreclosures" have become synonymous with great deals. However there are fundamental differences between them and it's important that you understand the differences before investing.

Caution: Remember that cheap does not always mean that it is a deal; it could be cheap for a bad reason. Always have an exit strategy in mind when you are buying.

Generally speaking there are three types of real estate transactions:

1. The traditional sale.

2. The short sale.

3. The foreclosure or sale of bank-owned property.

Let's briefly review each in the following sections.

2.1 The traditional sale

The traditional sale is likely the type of sale that you are used to if you have ever purchased a property. It involves two parties: the buyers and the sellers. The sellers may or may not have a mortgage on their property but the important thing to note is that the amount of the note or mortgage does not exceed the sale price of the property. In this case the sellers, at their sole discretion, can sell the property at the price that is convenient for them and do not need third party or lender approval to do so, because the proceeds from the sale more than cover all expenses including the repayment of the note.

2.2 The short sale

A short sale is unique in the sense that the seller of the property is facing financial distress and often he or she is late on mortgage payments because of any number of reasons, so is trying to sell the house for less money than is actually owed on the note or mortgage.

For example, Mr. and Mrs. Smith purchased their home at the height of the market in 2005 for $300,000. At the time they really could only afford a $200,000 home but they were lured into a five-year, interest-only loan that made them feel that they could afford a $300,000 home because of the low, interest-only payments. They proceeded to purchase their home with a zero percent downpayment and therefore owed the full $300,000 plus closing costs, for a total of about $310,000. The Smiths had opted for an Adjustable Rate Mortgage (ARM), where after five years the rate adjusted to prime + 5 percent. Fast forward five years: Mr. Smith loses his job and to make matters worse, his mortgage payments tripled overnight because of the adjustment in rate. Now the family definitely can't afford the new mortgage payments and are forced to sell their home. Unfortunately, because of the market conditions and declining property values, it would be impossible for them sell their house for the amount of the mortgage. Therefore, they are selling the property for a shortfall which constitutes a "short sale."

When you hear the term "being upside down," this is what's being referred to. Simplistically, a short sale is where there is a sale and the person owes more on the property than the property is worth.

You are probably wondering why this is relevant. Well it's important that as a buyer you understand that when you put an offer on the Smiths' residence, for example, you are in fact facing a situation where the sale is subject to third-party approval, i.e., that of the lender or lenders.

Here is how a short sale works: Like a traditional sale, you would put an offer on the property that interests you and request that the selling party accept the terms or price of the sale. So far it's the same process as a traditional sale. But now that you have placed your offer for the property, both the lender(s) and the owners must decide whether they will allow the property to be sold at this price or not. Remember, the lenders are potentially taking a large loss on this property (the difference between the outstanding mortgage and the sale price). This is the part that can be very time consuming and frustrating if you work with a realtor who does not understand the negotiation process and all of the things that need to be provided to the bank to help make the decision.

Now let's twist this situation slightly and assume for a second that two years after the property was purchased, the Smiths refinanced their home and took a second mortgage. Now both mortgagees need to agree to a payoff amount for the deal to happen since we know that there are not enough funds to cover both loans at the current purchase price. It is also important to note that both the first and second mortgage holders need to agree on a settlement before the short sale can be approved and the transaction can occur.

One more common caveat is when the mortgage holder requires the sellers to sign off on a personal promissory note. The reasons behind why it may or may not be required are complex and not important for you to understand; as the buyer, however, it is important for you to understand that this may delay the process.

These are two common reasons that short sales take time and require patience to get a final approval, but the time and frustration can be justified by the potential deal that one may get.

There are many realtors who think they understand this process, but few that have actually mastered it. Look for real estate professionals who have seen first-hand horror stories where clients purchased distressed properties; hopefully they can guide you through the numerous issues. The short sale negotiation process requires certain skills and methods to ensure smooth transactions, and thus it is important that you select the right real estate professional to represent you in this purchase.

Do not attempt this on your own. Certain key steps early in the process can help mitigate the time it takes to get the short sale approved and help avoid issues.

2.3 Foreclosure or bank-owned property

In simplistic terms a foreclosure is a property where the note bearer has forcefully evicted the inhabitants for nonpayment of their mortgages. If we take the previous example with the Smith family and assume they stopped paying the mortgage, eventually they would be driven out of their home and the bank would take over the property. Since lenders are not in the business of owning property, they proceed to sell the property in an as-is condition on the open market. Bank properties are often the fastest deals to close, but have their own challenges because they are often properties that have not been lived in for a while and therefore need attention to bring them up to a livable standard.

3. Currency

Table 2 shows the Canadian dollar expressed in US funds since 1950. The average over those 65 years is $0.8838. While the currencies were trading around par in 2011 and 2012, they were not at par for nearly 40 years prior to that.

I have many Canadians tell me how high the US dollar is (how low the Canadian dollar is) and that they would lose 20 percent if they invested in the US now. I want to make two points here;

1. From a historical perspective, the Canadian dollar is not that low compared to the US dollar.

2. A Canadian who converts his or her money to US dollars will not lose 20 percent (assuming an $0.80 dollar). If that statement were true, then it would follow that if

I converted US dollars to Canadian dollars, I would make 20 percent, but no one ever makes that claim. However, if A is true (losing money one direction), B must be true (making money the other direction). To carry this one step further, if losing or gaining money were actually possible I would turn all of my assets into Japanese Yen and become a billionaire. You do not lose money by converting currency from one to another (with the exception of any fees paid to banks or other convertors).

Note: You can lose money via a change in currency over time. For example, if I bought $100 CAD and converted it to $80 USD today and a week later, I converted the $80 USD back to Canadian dollars but only received $95 CAD, I would lose money. To summarize, you cannot lose money by exchanging it for another currency (ignoring the fee), but you can lose money for transactions that span a period of time because of exchange rate fluctuations.

Also keep in mind that you can have a gain on the real estate, but a loss on the currency exchange, or vice versa. Many people are surprised to find that they had a loss on their US real estate, but had gain to report in Canada due to the increase in the currency. Your gain or loss in Canada will have to account for the currency difference. For example, if you bought a home in 2010 for $200,000 USD when the currency was $0.97, it took $206,186 CAD to buy the house. If you sold the home in 2014 for $225,000 USD when the currency was at $0.91, you will have a $25,000 USD gain for US purposes and you would have converted the $225,000 USD into $247,253 CAD, for a gain of $41,067 CAD.

4. Before You Get Started

I would like to stress the importance of working with reputable real estate professionals. The professionals that you surround yourself with when making such an important decision can make a world of difference. Decisions are always better made when you are well informed of the process and it never hurts to be to be too well-informed, if there is such a thing.

Being well informed is more than finding the right property, in the right location, at the right price; you have to understand how best to take title to the property, what the tax implications are when you own and sell the property, and when you die. These items and more will be covered in the next chapters.

Table 2
Canadian Dollar in US Funds (Annual Average)

CANADIAN DOLLAR AS EXPRESSED IN US FUNDS
(AVERAGE ANNUAL)

1950 - $1.00 CDN = $0.9181 US	1983 - $1.00 CDN = $0.8115 US
1951 - " " = $0.9498 "	1984 - " " = $0.7723 "
1952 - " " = $1.0216 "	1985 - " " = $0.7325 "
1953 - " " = $1.0168 "	1986 - " " = $0.7197 "
1954 - " " = $1.0275 "	1987 - " " = $0.7542 "
1955 - " " = $1.0138 "	1988 - " " = $0.8124 "
1956 - " " = $1.0161 "	1989 - " " = $0.8444 "
1957 - " " = $1.0429 "	1990 - " " = $0.8570 "
1958 - " " = $1.0329 "	1991 - " " = $0.8727 "
1959 - " " = $1.0427 "	1992 - " " = $0.8276 "
1960 - " " = $1.0312 "	1993 - " " = $0.7726 "
1961 - " " = $0.9869 "	1994 - " " = $0.7293 "
1962 - " " = $0.9355 "	1995 - " " = $0.7284 "
1963 - " " = $0.9272 "	1996 - " " = $0.7334 "
1964 - " " = $0.9271 "	1997 - " " = $0.7225 "
1965 - " " = $0.9276 "	1998 - " " = $0.6743 "
1966 - " " = $0.9282 "	1999 - " " = $0.6766 "
1967 - " " = $0.9270 "	2000 - " " = $0.6793 "
1968 - " " = $0.9281 "	2001 - " " = $0.6458 "
1969 - " " = $0.9287 "	2002 - " " = $0.6368 "
1970 - " " = $0.9578 "	2003 - " " = $0.7135 "
1971 - " " = $0.9903 "	2004 - " " = $0.7683 "
1972 - " " = $1.0096 "	2005 - " " = $0.8253 "
1973 - " " = $0.9994 "	2006 - " " = $0.8818 "
1974 - " " = $1.0225 "	2007 - " " = $0.9304 "
1975 - " " = $0.9830 "	2008 - " " = $0.9381 "
1976 - " " = $0.9862 "	2009 - " " = $0.8757 "
1977 - " " = $0.9404 "	2010 - " " = $0.9709 "
1978 - " " = $0.8770 "	2011 - " " = $1.0110 "
1979 - " " = $0.8536 "	2012 - " " = $1.0004 "
1980 - " " = $0.8554 "	2013 - " " = $0.9710 "
1981 - " " = $0.8340 "	2014 - " " = $0.9054 "
1982 - " " = $0.8103 "	

2

Forms of Real Estate Ownership and Factors to Consider when Choosing

When buying real estate in the US, there are two ways in which title can be taken: directly by the individual or indirectly through some sort of entity such as a corporation. You can further divide indirect ownership into Canadian entities and US entities.

In this chapter, I will be discussing different forms of ownership, as well as the pros and cons of each. In general, the three most important factors to consider in deciding on a form of ownership are:

- Whether there are any tax benefits.

- How to limit liability.

- How to limit costs and hassles.

Each form of ownership will have a combination of tax efficiency, liability exposure, costs, and hassles. It is very important to balance each of these factors and not place too much or too little emphasis on each factor.

One more factor to consider when deciding on a form of ownership is whether the property will be sold quickly (fix and flip), or held long-term (perhaps rented out). If you will have a mixture of rentals and flips, you may want two different ownership structures for each type of strategy.

1. Types of Ownership

1.1 Direct ownership

The simplest way to buy a piece of real estate is to title the property directly in your name or you and your spouse or partner's name. Of course, direct ownership is not limited to two people or to a husband and wife; there can be many individuals named on the title. While it is possible to name any number of individuals on the title, I would typically recommend establishing some sort of entity rather than an individual, if you name anyone other than a spouse or partner.

If you are considering naming a child co-owner to avoid probate, 26 states plus the District of Columbia allow for the property to be transferred on death directly to a beneficiary without probate (see Table 3). This is also known as Transfer on Death deed, or a beneficiary deed. A beneficiary deed is similar to any other beneficiary designation you use such as with your registered accounts or with life insurance. The beneficiary can be changed at any time before death. If the property is held jointly, the beneficiary automatically receives the property after the second person's death. A beneficiary deed can be done on your own or with an attorney and the cost is minimal.

If you own property in Florida, Michigan, or Texas, an enhanced life estate (a.k.a., Lady Bird Deed), might make sense for you. Life estates and enhanced life estates are discussed in more detail in section 1.1b.

Table 3
States That Allow Transfer on Death (TOD), a.k.a., Beneficiary Deed

Alaska	Arizona	Arkansas	California	Colorado
District of Columbia	Hawaii	Illinois	Indiana	Kansas
Minnesota	Missouri	Montana	Nebraska	Nevada
New Mexico	North Dakota	Ohio	Oklahoma	Oregon
South Dakota	Texas	Virginia	Washington	West Virginia
Wisconsin	Wyoming			

1.1a   The type of ownership depends on the state

Not all states allow all possible ways to own a property. In general, there are two types of laws in which to own property; they are called community property states and common law states. Community property states are: Arizona, California, Idaho, Louisiana, Nevada, New Mexico, Texas, Washington, and Wisconsin. Below are some basic definitions of the different ways to own property directly.

Individual Ownership (Fee Simple): A fee simple represents absolute ownership of land, and therefore the owner may do whatever he or she chooses with the land. If an owner of a fee simple dies intestate (without a will), the land will descend to the heirs, subject to probate unless other measures are taken.

Joint tenancy: The most common way for couples to own property is as joint tenants. This means that each person owns an equal share in the property. If one owner dies, the survivor will then own the entire property by "rights of survivorship." The surviving joint tenant receives the property automatically. This means that the property will avoid the probate process and the associated fees.

Community property: In community property states only, married couples can take ownership as community property. In this case, they will each own a half-interest in the property. Unlike joint tenants, the owners can pass their interest (half) by will or trust upon their death and will not avoid probate.

Community property with rights of survivorship: Certain community property states allow married couples to own property as community property with rights of survivorship. Like community property, the couple will each own a half-interest in the property, however when one of them dies the survivor automatically owns the entire property and avoids probate.

Tenancy by the entirety (a.k.a., tenants by entirety): In about half of the states (25 plus the District of Columbia) (see Table 4), married couples can own property as tenants by entirety. Like joint tenants, this form of ownership means that the surviving spouse owns the entire property and avoids probate. The primary difference between tenancy by entirety and joint tenancy is that joint tenants may deal with the property as they wish. If one joint tenant decides to convey his or her interest in the property, that interest is conveyed, and the joint tenancy is destroyed. In tenancy by entirety, each tenant effectively owns the entire estate. Therefore, neither can deal with the property independently of the other.

Tenancy by entirety provides a certain level of asset protection due to the fact that neither partner is able to act without the consent of the other; meaning that if one spouse is sued, the creditor cannot force the other spouse to surrender the property.

Tenancy in common: Multiple owners can be listed as tenants in common. These owners can divide their interests in unequal percentages such as 80/20. The property does not avoid probate.

The two most common ways for spouses to own property directly are either joint tenants or community property with rights of survivorship. In both cases the property passes to the surviving spouse and avoids probate. There are some differences in the rights of spouses, so if this is a concern, please consult an attorney for the specific differences.

Table 4
States that Allow Ownership as Tenants by Entirety

Alaska	Arkansas	Delaware	District of Columbia	Florida
Hawaii	*Illinois*	*Indiana*	*Kentucky*	Michigan
Maryland	Massachusetts	Mississippi	Missouri	*New Jersey*
New York	*North Carolina*	Oklahoma	*Oregon*	Pennsylvania
Rhode Island	Tennessee	Vermont	Virginia	Wyoming

States in italics allow Tenants by Entirety for real estate only; all other states allow Tenants by Entirety for any asset.

When buying in a community property state, owning the property as community property with rights of survivorship is typically preferable for two reasons and they both have to do with how the property is taxed at death (Internal Revenue Code 2040): If the property is owned as joint tenants or as tenancy by the entirety, the deceased is presumed to have owned 100 percent of the property. Assuming the first to die owned twice the amount of assets in the US at death (100 percent versus 50 percent), it may cause the deceased to be subject to US nonresident estate tax. While this presumption can be refuted, it can be a time-consuming and costly process, at a very distressful time. Community property ownership does not have this presumption, which means the first to die is treated as owning 50 percent of the property, and therefore things go much more smoothly at the first death.

When a couple owns property as joint tenants and one spouse dies, that person's cost basis in their half of the property gets adjusted to fair market value (FMV) at the date of death. However, couples owning property as community property with rights of survivorship will have the cost basis adjusted on both halves (the deceased and the survivor's) adjusted to FMV.

Basic scenario: John and Carol Smith bought a house for $200,000. This means that essentially they bought the house for $100,000 each. Five years later John dies when the house is worth $300,000. On the date of death they owned a property worth $150,000 to each of them and each of them had a cost basis of $100,000, giving them each a gain of $50,000.

Joint tenants scenario: If the home was purchased as joint tenants with rights of survivorship, only John's half of the home would be adjusted to FMV. This means that the half Carol receives from John has its cost basis adjusted from $100,000 to $150,000. Carol continues to retain her cost basis of $100,000. She now owns the entire property worth $300,000, with a cost basis of $250,000 (Carol's $100,000 plus John's $150,000). If Carol were to sell the home immediately, she would have a $50,000 gain, ignoring selling costs.

Community property scenario: If the home was purchased as community property with rights of survivorship, each of their halves would be adjusted at the first death. This means that Carol would inherit the property with a $300,000 cost basis (FMV = $300,000 and basis is adjusted to FMV). This wipes out all capital gains as of John's death. If Carol were to sell the home immediately, she would incur no capital gains, ignoring selling costs. Of course, any appreciation from the date of death forward would be subject to tax when Carol sells the property, in both scenarios.

Caution: If the property declines in value, the cost basis also declines. In the above community property example, if the property declined to $150,000 at John's death, Carol would inherit the property with a basis of $150,000 – a loss of basis of $50,000. If they owned the property as joint tenants, the basis would be $175,000; John's half adjusted to $75,000 and Carol would retain her $100,000 basis.

Life estate: This is a kind of joint ownership of real estate. A life estate is defined as an estate whose duration is limited to the life of the party holding it, or some other person.

A life estate enables you to sell or gift your home to your children (or anyone else), but keep the right to live in or control the home until you die. When you do this, you keep a "life estate." When you have a life estate, you are called the life tenant and your child (or other person) is called the remainderman. It is possible to give more than one child or person a remainder interest in your home, in which case they would be called remaindermen.

While a life estate may seem appealing at first blush, there are five main problems with this type of ownership:

1. You cannot easily obtain a mortgage on the property. The remaindermen, typically your children and their spouses, must all agree in writing to borrow against the property. You cannot remove their names from the title unless they agree and you cannot force them to agree.

2. You cannot sell the property without the consent of remaindermen; typically your children and their spouses. Since the remaindermen own an interest in the property, they could demand a share of the proceeds if you sell it. This is true even if you gave (gifted) the property to them by adding their names to the title without receiving any money from them for their interest.

3. Your condo or homeowners' association, if applicable, may require that you obtain approval.

4. Selling the home could cause tax problems for you and your remaindermen. This is true even if your remaindermen sell the house after your death. Adding someone's name to the title of your home may be a gift under tax law, and a gift tax return may need to be filed. If the remaindermen sell the house after you die, they might have to pay capital gains tax on the proceeds. Note that according to US tax law, if you hold the property until your death, the capital gain completely disappears.

5. Once the remaindermen are on the deed to your property they have an interest in the property and their legal problems could become yours. If any of your remaindermen are sued or have to file for bankruptcy, a lien could be filed

against your home. The lien would have to be paid if you wanted to sell or mortgage the property. Your remainder-men's interest in the home is not protected if they file for bankruptcy. If any of your remaindermen gets divorced, his or her spouse could claim all or part of the remainder-man's interest in your home. If any of the remaindermen die before you do, your estate would have to go through probate. Your remaindermen should have a will saying what should happen to their interest in your home in this situation.

Enhanced life estate: An enhanced life estate (Lady Bird deed) is a form of deed that, like a traditional life estate deed, allows property to pass automatically to one or more designated recipients at death, without the need for probate. As of this writing, only Florida, Michigan, and Texas recognize Lady Bird deeds.

A Lady Bird deed could be a quitclaim deed, general warranty deed, or special warranty deed. I recommend that you do not use a quitclaim deed because it provides no protection for claims or confusions over the title to your property; I recommend using either a general or special warranty deed to protect your title.

1.1b   Advantages of Lady Bird deeds over traditional life estate deeds

Once a traditional life estate deed is signed, the grantor cannot sell, mortgage, convey, gift, or otherwise terminate the remainder interest during his or her lifetime without the consent of the remainder beneficiaries. In other words, the current owner cannot change his or her mind without involving the remaindermen. Lady Bird deeds are intended to avoid this problem.

Like a traditional life estate deed, a Lady Bird deed allows you to name someone to receive the property at your death while reserving the right to use the property during your lifetime, however, unlike a traditional life estate deed you are able to deal with the property during your lifetime, without the consent of the remainder beneficiaries.

Lady Bird deeds may allow you to:

- Keep complete control of the property during your lifetime without requiring consent of the remainder beneficiaries.

- Retain the right to use, profit from, or sell the property during your lifetime.

- Avoid triggering the federal gift tax on the transfer during your lifetime.

- Avoid probate of the property at your death.

However, if your remaindermen have any income tax liens, judgments, or bankruptcies, they may have to be paid off before the property can be sold; alternatively the creditor may be entitled to a portion of the property. Note that there are differences of opinion on this point. Please seek legal counsel before using either type of deed.

1.2 Indirect ownership

If you do not own the property in your own name, by definition you own the property indirectly. Examples of indirect ownership include corporations, partnerships, trusts, and hybrid entities that can be treated like a corporation, partnership, or sole proprietorship.

There are two main reasons for using an entity. The first reason is to protect your assets from lawsuits or other creditors. The second reason to use an entity is to avoid disputes when there are individuals other than spouses/partners with ownership in the same asset or business. Whenever there are owners with different economic interests, the likelihood of a dispute increases substantially. In these situations, an entity and the corresponding agreement would address who has what authority, which items require a vote, etc., which would serve to minimize, if not eliminate disputes.

2. Protecting Your Assets

The number one reason for establishing an entity to own your US property is to protect your assets from creditors, but an entity is more costly to establish and to maintain than simply owning the property directly; is it worth it?

As a reminder, I am not an attorney and legal advice should be sought before making a final decision, but I will attempt to lay out the issues for you to consider.

According to some sources, the US is the most litigious country in the world. According to other sources, most individuals and business owners have not been sued. However, just as you don't forgo buying fire insurance on your home just because a fire is not likely, you should not forgo forming an entity to minimize your liability just because you are not likely to be sued. You should buy insurance to avoid the devastating financial impact in case of a fire; likewise, a person could form an entity to avoid the devastation of any lawsuit that may be successful.

2.1 US homestead exemptions

Many people have heard of homestead exemptions, especially in Florida, and have asked about them, so I am including a few comments. The most important thing to know about homestead exemptions is that they only apply to a person's principal residence. At a minimum, you have to be a resident of the state and it has to be the home where you spend the majority of your time. While the US home may not be your principal residence now, you may be considering making it your principal residence at some point in the future.

The details of the homestead exemption vary from state to state, but typically have these features in common:

- Provides some protection from creditors (except mortgages, mechanics' liens, or property taxes).

- Provides some amount of reduction in property taxes.

The degree and amount of protection varies from state to state. For example, Texas and Florida have no dollar limit on the exemption. There are limits as to the size of the homestead, however. For example, Texas limits the urban homestead exemption to ten acres. In these states, if you are sued for other than for nonpayment of your mortgage, property taxes, or for a mechanic's lien, your home is protected even if it is worth $10 million, $100 million, or more.

California protects up to $75,000 for a single person or $100,000 for married couples, or $175,000 for people over 65 and the legally disabled. Arizona provides a $150,000 exemption, whether married or not.

Texas, Florida, and California homesteads also provide reductions in property taxes.

3. Pros and Cons of Different Entities (As It Relates to Canadians Buying US Real Estate)

In this section, I will explain some of the pros and cons of owning US real estate in three different types of Canadian entities: corporations, partnerships, and trusts. The most important thing to remember is that what works in Canada may not work in the US and what works in the US may not work in Canada. Table 5 summarizes the pros and cons of each ownership type.

Caution: Don't assume the rules are the same in both countries; typically they are not.

Note: If your assets exceed the US exemption amount ($5,450,000 USD in 2016), you may be subject to US nonresident estate tax. This tax can be completely avoided if the US property is properly owned through a foreign (Canadian) entity. For more on the US nonresident estate tax and how to avoid it, see Chapter 4: Nonresident US Estate Tax and Probate.

Table 5
Summary of the Pros and Cons of Ownership Types*

Type of Ownership	Pros	Cons	Conclusion
Direct Ownership			
Community Property	Simple, no cost, potential capital gain tax advantage at death, bank financing available	Probate expenses, only available in certain states, no liability protection	Community property with rights of survivorship is typically preferred where available
Community Property with Rights of Survivorship	Simple, no cost, potential capital gain tax advantage at first death, no probate expenses, avoids presumption that deceased owned 100%	Must pass directly to surviving spouse, only available in nine states, no liability protection	Where direct ownership is desired, preferred where available
Joint Tenants with Rights of Survivorship	Simple, no cost, can be used with non-spouse and multiple owners	No potential capital gain advantage at death, no liability protection, deceased is presumed to own 100% at death	Where direct ownership is desired and community property is not available, typically the preferred choice
Tenants by Entirety	Simple, no cost, potential asset protection, avoids presumption the deceased owned 100% at death	No potential capital gain advantage at death, not available in every state	Viable alternative to joint tenancy with rights of survivorship in states that allow it
Tenants in common	Simple, no cost, can be used with non-spouse and multiple owners	No potential capital gain advantage at death, no liability protection	Preferred when direct ownership is desired and a couple is not married according to US law
Indirect Ownership			
Canadian Coporation	Avoids US nonresident estate tax	Higher taxes, costs, complexity, personal use issues, difficulty obtaining financing	Recommended in very limited situations

Table 5 — Continued

Canadian Limited Partnership	Avoid US nonresident estate tax	Costs, complexity, personal use issues, difficulty obtaining financing	Generally preferred method to avoid US nonresident estate tax
Canadian Irrevocable Trust	Avoid US nonresident estate tax	Costs, complexity, 21-year deemed disposition, personal use issues, and difficulty obtaining financing	Avoids US nonresident estate tax, but Canadian limited partnership is typically a better option
US Limited Liability Company (LLC)	Asset protection	Costs, complexity, higher taxes, difficulty obtaining financing	Never use
US Corporation	Asset protection	Costs, complexity, higher taxation, personal use issues, difficulty obtaining financing	Recommended in very limited situations and in conjunction with a Canadian Corporation
US Revocable Trust	Avoids probate	Cost to establish, no asset protection, complexity	There are much better ways to avoid probate; don't use
US Limited Liability Parthership (LLP)	Asset protection, no double taxation	Costs, complexity, difficulty obtaining financing	When asset protection is desired, preferred method if no need or desire for limited partners
US Limited Liability Limited Partnership (LLLP)	Asset protection, no double taxation	Costs, complexity, difficulty obtaining financing	When asset protection is desired, preferred method for those with a need or desire for limited partners

* Assuming Canadian residency.

3.1 Canadian entities

3.1a Canadian corporations

Canadian corporations have been one of the most commonly suggested ways of owning US real estate. I believe this is due to the fact that the use of a Canadian corporation is familiar and convenient. In addition, if the corporation were appropriate, it would save the cost of forming an additional entity to own the property. However, there are some significant reasons not to use a Canadian corporation when buying US real estate. The disadvantages are that it will cause double taxation, and generally eliminate the possibility of special capital gains tax treatment.

A Canadian corporation doing business in the US will have to file IRS Form 1120-F : US Income Tax Return of a Foreign Corporation. US tax law imposes a double tax on corporations because the income is taxed within the corporation and any dividends paid to shareholders are not deductible by the corporation (first tax), then the shareholders have to pay tax on the dividend they receive (second tax).

Another issue is that single-purpose corporations are not allowed to own real estate. If you do own an older Canadian corporation that allows for the ownership of real estate, you still need to be careful to follow the rules so that your corporation does not become a disallowed entity. This can happen if your corporation owns a home in which you live in (or otherwise receive personal benefits) and you do not pay fair market rent to the corporation or take into income the value of the fair market rent. In other words, even if you do not pay fair market rent to the corporation, fair market rent will be imputed to the corporation. All in all, with some rare exceptions, I do not recommend buying US real estate in a Canadian (or US) corporation.

3.1b Canadian corporation with US subsidiary corporation

Canadian corporations with US subsidiary corporations are sometimes recommended because the Treaty allows the dividend payment from the US Corporation to the Canadian Corporation to be made with only a 5 percent withholding tax applied. If the Canadian Corporation held the US property directly, a 15 percent withholding tax would be required.

Foreign Accrual Property Income (FAPI): Previous to 1976, Canadian corporations with foreign affiliates were able to keep foreign passive income from being taxed in Canada until the profits were repatriated back into Canada. To prevent wealthy Canadians from establishing foreign holding companies to hold their investment assets and avoid Canadian tax indefinitely, Canada implemented foreign affiliate rules in 1976. FAPI does not apply to active business income.

The most common sources of foreign accrual property income (passive income) are:

- Income from a portfolio of investments — interest and dividends.
- Rental income.
- Capital gains, not considered part of an active business.

These activities are called investment businesses, to separate them from active businesses. It is possible that an investment can meet the threshold of an active business if either an activity or number of employees test is met. Meeting the requirements for an active business would be the exception so I will not spend any more time on this issue. If you feel that your rental activities may qualify as an active business, please consult your tax advisor for the requirements and their advice.

If a Canadian corporation (parent) has a foreign affiliate (sub), the parent must include its portion of the passive income earned by the sub on its tax return, whether or not the passive income was distributed to the parent.

Note: FAPI only applies to Canadian corporations with foreign affiliates; Canadian corporations that directly hold US real estate are not subject to FAPI rules.

3.1c   Canadian Limited Partnership

This is a common way for sophisticated Canadian investors to buy real estate in Canada, but few Canadians own a Limited Partnership. While a Canadian Limited Partnership could work in buying US property, there are some reasons that I would not suggest their use, especially if you don't already have one.

If you are doing business in the US it is better to have an entity in the state in which you own the property in case legal issues arise, rather than trying to have a Canadian attorney learn local laws. Another matter that arises occasionally is the confusion or even outright refusal to work with a foreign entity, not because of some sort of prejudice, but because of fear of the unknown. Rather than learn the differences in the rules when dealing with a foreign entity, some take the path of least resistance and refuse to work with the foreign entity.

3.1d   Canadian Limited Liability Partnership (LLP)

An LLP offers the partners limited liability in that the partners are only liable up to their contribution (amount invested) into the partnership. An LLP differs from a traditional partnership, where all of the partners are liable for acts of all of the partners. In traditional limited partnerships, at least one of the partners has liability for the acts of the other partners, and at least one of the partners has limited liability.

Traditionally, a Canadian LLP is limited to professionals such as attorneys. However, British Columbia has an LLP that can be used for any legal business purpose. Also, anyone in any province, can use a BC LLP.

BC LLPs are required to file an annual report with the BC Corporate Registry and submit annual Partnership Information Returns to the Canadian Revenue Agency which state the partners' share of the profits and losses of the LLP.

The income and losses from a BC LLP flow through to the individual partners. Assuming the partners are individuals, the tax consequences will be the same as if the individual owned the property directly. The BC LLP is a good option for Canadian investors.

3.1e A Canadian trust

A Canadian Trust is the least popular way for a Canadian to buy real estate. The reason someone would consider using a Canadian trust is to avoid US nonresident estate tax. However, there are good reasons for not using a trust and they are higher tax rates and a deemed sale every 21 years.

To avoid the US nonresident estate tax, an irrevocable trust would have to be used. This means that you would have to give up all control over the assets in the trust; you have to essentially give the assets away. Granted that the beneficiaries of the trust could be your heirs, but for most people, giving those assets away while they are alive, is not an option. If a trust sounds like a viable solution for you, I recommend the cross-border irrevocable trust.

Note: While a BC LLP may be a good choice, Canadian corporations, limited partnerships, and Canadian trusts are generally not recommended for buying US real estate, though a strategy using a Canadian two-tiered limited partnership can be used to avoid US nonresident estate tax.

3.2 US entities

3.2a Limited Liability Company (LLC)

Commonly used by Americans to purchase real estate, LLCs are occasionally, but incorrectly, recommended to Canadians buying real estate in the US. The fundamental problem with Canadians using LLCs is that the US and Canada treat LLCs differently. An LLC is a hybrid entity, meaning that in the US it can be treated as a partnership, a corporation, or if there is a single member (partner), the LLC will be treated as if there is no entity at all. In this situation the LLC is referred to as a disregarded entity. However, Canada treats an LLC as a corporation.

In the US the LLC will nearly always be taxed as a partnership, which means that the income will flow through to the partners each year regardless of whether a distribution was made. This of course means that tax will be applied each year as the profit is earned. Since Canada treats the LLC as a corporation, no Canadian income will be reported until there is a distribution. Because US and Canadian taxes are paid in different years, the foreign tax credit mechanism does not work and there is a double tax. The problems with treating the LLC as a corporation will be discussed next.

As a member of an LLC you will typically choose to be taxed as a partnership and be required to file a Partnership return (Form 1065), and an individual nonresident alien tax return (Form 1040NR). You may also be required to file a separate state income tax return.

Caution: An LLC is the worst way for a Canadian to purchase US real estate. If you have already used an LLC to purchase US real estate, consult a cross-border tax professional about the best way to correct the situation.

3.2b US corporations

US corporations can be used in certain limited situations, but in general should be avoided when buying US real estate as a Canadian. Unlike in Canada, there are very few good reasons for having a US corporation for any business except for the very largest; the reason is double taxation. Money earned in a corporation is taxed once at the corporate level and once again at the individual level. Because there is no dividend credit similar to what is provided in Canada, the income is simply taxed twice. Another reason a corporation is typically avoided is the loss of the preferential capital gains tax rate within a corporation. A US or Canadian Corporation is a bad way to purchase real estate in the US.

As a shareholder of a US Corporation, you would be required to file a US Corporate income tax return (Form 1120). You may also be required to file a separate state income tax return.

3.2c Revocable living trust (or simply living trust)

Living trusts can provide a number of benefits in the right circumstances. The circumstance where the living trust is best is where you are buying a second home. If there will be any business activity such as a rental, then a different entity should be considered to help protect you from personal liability. When considering a living trust (or any other entity) it is frequently simply a matter of cost versus benefit.

The only reason to use a living trust is to avoid the cost of probate. Probate involves a cost of settling your estate. Any assets that have to be passed to your heirs via your will are subject to probate. A living trust allows the asset to pass directly to your heirs and avoids your will and therefore probate. You have to weigh the cost of establishing the trust versus the cost of probate. In most states, probate cannot easily be avoided by other means. However, as I mentioned earlier when talking about direct ownership, 24 states and the District of Columbia allow real estate to be transferred on death directly to the beneficiary (via beneficiary deed). If the beneficiary deed is used, a trust is not needed to avoid probate.

Note: If a living trust seems appropriate and you are considering its use, then I recommend that you look into a cross-border trust instead to address the foreign trust issues.

3.2d Limited Liability Partnership (LLP) and Limited Liability Limited Partnership (LLLP)

An LLP is essentially a general partnership that provides limited liability to the partners. A Limited Liability Limited Partnership (LLLP) is a limited partnership that provides limited liability to the general partner.

As a member of an LLP or LLLP you will be required to file a Partnership return: Form 1065, and an individual nonresident alien tax return: Form 1040NR. You may also be required to file separate provincial and state income tax returns. Any tax you pay

Figure 1
Basic Decision Tree

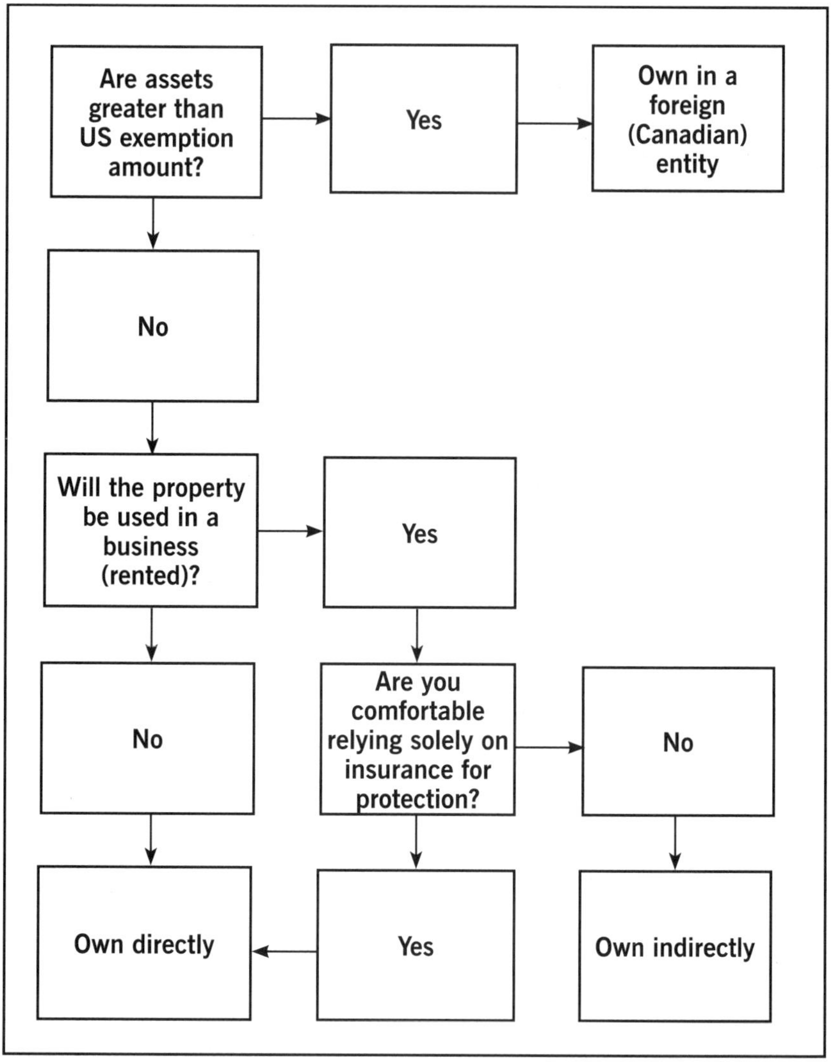

| Are assets greater than US exemption amount? | → | Yes | → | Own in a foreign (Canadian) entity |

No
↓

| Will the property be used in a business (rented)? | → | Yes |

No
↓

Are you comfortable relying solely on insurance for protection? → No

| Own directly | ← | Yes | | Own indirectly |

as part of your 1040NR filing can be used as a credit against your Canadian income tax.

Important: These are entities which have frequently been recommended (including by me) when buying US real estate that will be turned into rentals. However, CRA has since stated that

US LLPs and LLLPs will be classified as corporations in Canada. This means that LLPs and LLLPs should not be used by Canadians.

The CRA realizes that their ruling will create a significant hardship on many Canadian taxpayers that have already formed US LLPs and LLLPs. They have announced that they will provide a transition period that will allow conversion of existing entities to another entity that the CRA recognizes as a partnership. To be eligible for this transition period, you must have formed the LLP or LLLP before July 2016; each of the partners must have treated the entity as a partnership for Canadian tax purposes; and the LLP or LLLP must be converted to a CRA recognized partnership no later than 2018.

4. Owning Multiple US Properties

Unfortunately there is no easy answer to what an investor should do when he or she is looking to invest in multiple US properties. Before it became clear that LLCs could not be used by Canadians even as disregarded entities owned by a US entity such as an LLP or LLLP, I frequently recommended that an investor establish a US LLP or LLLP and have that entity be the only owner of multiple LLCs. Back then, a single-member LLC would be established for every property or every couple of properties, which would limit the liability to the value of the assets in any one LLC. The other advantage is that none of those LLCs would require a tax return be filed.

Today I do not recommend Canadians use an LLC, US LLP, or LLLP in any circumstance, and if you already have one of these you should talk to your advisor about the possibility of moving out of that structure into one that is more tax-efficient. Today the choices are:

- holding the properties in your own name,

- placing all of the properties in one entity, or

- establishing multiple entities for multiple properties.

Most people opt for either placing all of the properties into one entity or establishing multiple entities. The decision comes down to how risk averse are you and how much money you want to spend protecting yourself in case of a lawsuit.

If you place all of your assets into one entity, you subject all of the assets in that entity to collections or seizure if someone associated with one of those properties decides to sue you. In other words, if you have three properties, A, B, and C, and someone in property A successfully sues you for an amount that exceeds the amount of insurance, the creditor may not only seize property A, but B and C as well. The creditor cannot come after any other assets; once the money runs out in the entity, the creditor is done. If you had properties A, B, and C in three different entities, then if the tenant in property A successfully sued you, he or she would be limited to the amount of the insurance, plus property A (and any money that is in the bank account); B and C would be protected.

Using the scenario above, if you created three entities and placed each property into a different entity, your expenses would be substantially higher than if you had only one entity. Assuming you used three LPs, you would have the expense of creating four entities (estimated $750 to $1,500 each) and an annual expense of three partnership returns (and one corporate return). Tax preparation would be approximately three times as expensive as preparing one return with all three properties because no scale can be achieved. So if it would cost you $2,000 to have one partnership return filed for three properties, you would most likely be looking at only $5,000 to have three separate partnership returns prepared.

This is one of those areas that professionals cannot give you specific advice, other than to say that if you will not be able to sleep knowing you might lose all of your US properties if you place them all into one entity, then the extra expense may be worth it to you. However, if you can live with more risk, the right decision for you might be to place all of the properties into one entity and spend a few hundred dollars more (rather than a few thousand dollars) and get $5 million of liability insurance rather than $1 million.

5. Investors with Worldwide Assets Greater Than the US Exemption Amount

Whether you are buying a second home or buying investment property, you could be subject to US nonresident estate tax on your US property if your worldwide assets exceed the US exemption amount of $5.45 million USD in 2016. The exemption amount is adjusted for inflation each year.

Please read Chapter 4 for all of the interesting details of US nonresident estate tax. In this chapter, I discuss the nonresident estate tax can be avoided if the US property is owned by certain foreign (non-US) entities.

Generally speaking an entity is considered as being located in (having *situs* is the legal term) the country to which it is subject to its laws; typically this would be the country where the entity was formed and the person forming the entity resides. There are basically three entity choices; corporation, irrevocable trust, and certain partnership structures.

Caution: Because of the complexity of this topic, you should definitely seek competent cross-border advice before doing anything in this area. Some additional details are provided in Chapter 4. I will not rehash the pros and cons of these different entity types when it comes to owning US real estate, instead I will discuss the strategy that I believe is the best course of action for most people. Please seek professional tax advice before employing any strategy.

Going forward, here is a definition of the terms:

- **Limited Partnership (LP):** Two or more partners united to conduct a business jointly, where at least one partner is the general partner and at least one partner is a limited partner.

- **General Partner (GP):** Owner that has unlimited liability. The general partner has the authority to make decisions, sign contracts, and bind the business, without the knowledge or permission of the limited partners.

- **Limited Partner (LP):** Owner that has limited liability to the extent of ownership. Limited partners do not have any kind of management responsibility and cannot make decisions on behalf of the business.

- **Canadian corporation:** A corporation formed in Canada and the majority of its voting shares are owned by residents of Canada. Since the Canadian corporation will be the general partner and therefore have unlimited liability, make sure the corporation owns as small a percentage as possible and has very few assets in it. I have seen people use one of their existing corporations with significant assets in it. Having significant assets in the corporation that is the GP defeats the purpose of having a corporation absorb any possible liability. If successfully sued, the assets of the corporation would be available to settle any award given to a plaintiff. This structure is the most tax-efficient structure that can keep your assets out of the US estate tax system because any income flows through to the individual partners and the foreign tax credit mechanism can be used to prevent double tax. While the income flowing to the corporation will be subject to double tax, the tax should be *de minimus*. If the corporation's ownership is limited to 1 percent or less, even with $100,000 of gross income, the income flowing to the corporation would only be $1,000 and if the tax on $1,000 is $100, doubled makes $200; $200 on $100,000 of income is only 0.2 percent.

If multiple US properties are contemplated then you have the same decision to make as discussed under section 4. The properties can all go into the US limited partnership, or multiple US limited partnerships can be formed.

A two-tiered limited partnership will likely be the way to go for most people. The illustration in Figure 2 lays out the structure.

Figure 2
Two-Tiered Limited Partnership

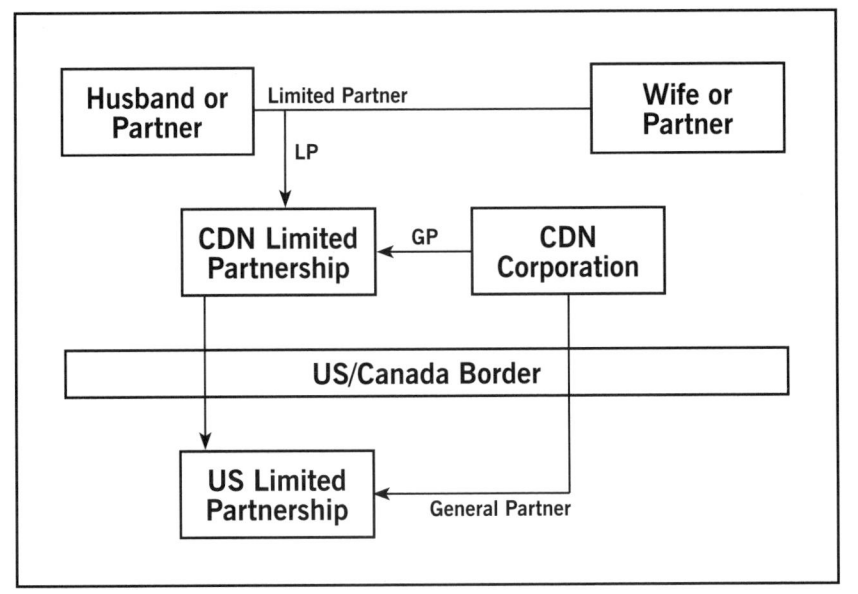

3

Income Taxes

As I discussed in Chapter 2, how you own the property may have a significant effect on how you are ultimately taxed. Different ways of owning the property can lead to different tax outcomes.

There are a number of issues to be considered when it comes to income taxes. Not only is there income tax on rent, but there is a capital gains tax on the sale, the availability of foreign tax credits, and the tax filing requirements, to name the most important considerations. There is also potential US nonresident estate tax that has to be considered; however, we'll save that discussion for Chapter 4.

1. The Basics

Many of the people I talk to have the same question: "Will having rental income in the US cause my worldwide income to be taxable in the US?" The answer is absolutely not! The nonresident tax system is designed to tax nonresident companies and individuals on their US income only. Likewise, dying with US real estate will not subject your entire estate to US estate taxes ("death taxes").

One thing that is important to remember as you think about US tax, as a Canadian, is that there are two different sources of laws that everyone must consider. The first set of laws is the Internal Revenue Code (IRC). Similar to the Income Tax Act (ITA) in Canada, the IRC is the set of laws that dictates the who, what, when, and how of taxes in the US.

The second set of laws is the US-Canada Tax Convention (Treaty). Some of the more important benefits the Treaty provides include reducing or eliminating double taxation, identifying which country has taxing priority, improved compliance with tax laws, and creating consistency while improving certainty for taxpayers with international dealings.

Because the purpose of the Treaty is to modify when, how and if certain income will be taxed, it is natural that there will be differences between the IRC and the Treaty; this is where much of the confusion comes from. The IRC is the default law and as a taxpayer you must elect to take advantage of the various Treaty provisions you wish to benefit from. In most situations, you will want to make those elections because it is beneficial to be taxed according to the Treaty. For example, the IRC stipulates that a 30 percent withholding tax rate applies to gross rental income earned in the US by nonresident aliens. The US-Canada Treaty allows you to take advantage of lower withholding on rents by having the net income (profits) subject to tax at US marginal rates, rather than 30 percent tax on the gross income.

There may be times when the Treaty and the IRC conflict, in which case the long-standing policy of the US is to settle the issue by using the "last in line" philosophy. Last in line means the last law to have been passed rules the day. The theory is that lawmakers, when passing the new law, took into consideration all of the issues and potential conflicts and decided this current law being passed is the latest and greatest thinking on the issue, and therefore takes precedent over any other law on the same subject.

For example, a few years ago, taxpayers that had foreign tax credits, and were subject to the Alternative Minimum Tax (AMT), were only able to reduce their regular tax liability by a maximum of 90 percent. As mentioned before, one of the main objectives of the Treaty is to avoid double taxation. To the extent taxpayers were subject to this AMT limitation on foreign tax credits there was double taxation. There was some question as to which law took precedent. As it turned out, the AMT law had been passed after the last amendment to the Treaty, therefore the double tax stood as the correct legal answer.

The IRS talks about income that is effectively connected with a trade or business. Throughout the IRC and the Treaty, you will see the term "effectively connected income," without the words "trade or business" connected to it. Whenever you see or hear someone talk about effectively connected income, know that they mean from a trade or business. Rental income is an example of effectively connected income.

It is not my intention to cover every possible scenario in this chapter or even in this book; my intention is to illustrate only the situations most Canadians will encounter. Consult Internal Revenue Service Publication 515 — Withholding of Tax on Nonresident Aliens and Foreign Entities, or consult a US-Canada tax specialist if you have a situation that is not covered in this book.

2. Rental Income
2.1 Rental income under direct ownership

If you were to own a rental property directly in your name or jointly with another person, the IRS specified withholding rate is 30 percent on the gross revenue of the rental activity. Revenue is defined as the gross amounts of money coming into the business before any expenses are taken. However, the Treaty allows you to elect to be taxed on the profit of the rental business instead of withholding on the gross income. Profit is defined as revenue less expenses. Non-accountants many times refer to profit as income or net income.

As a nonresident owner of a rental property, you will normally hire a property manager to take care of the day-to-day activities of the rental operations. The property manager will be your US withholding agent and as such will be required to withhold the necessary tax. When searching for property managers, be sure the manager understands his or her obligation to withhold and how to complete the necessary forms.

There are many peculiarities in the US tax system and two of them apply in the case of withholding on rentals. If you do not hire a property manager, technically your tenant is the withholding agent. Publication 515 (Withholding of Tax on Nonresident Aliens and Foreign Entities) states "Generally, the US person who pays an amount subject to nonresident alien (NRA) withholding is the person responsible for withholding." This is peculiar primarily because this places the tenant in a potentially adversarial role with you, the owner. If I were a tenant, I would not want to be personally liable for the withholding tax, nor would I want to spend my time learning the applicable laws and filing the necessary tax forms, or spend the money to hire an accountant. Nonetheless, from a legal point of view, that is the position the tenant would be in. The other peculiarity is that while you are allowed to file an election to be taxed on your profits (net income), that election is made when you file your US tax return, Form 1040NR, sometime the following year. Yet, the withholding agent is generally required to withhold 30 percent of the rent amount from each payment, barring an election to the contrary. Because Form 1040NR is not required to be filed for six and a half days after the end of the year, in a worst-case scenario, 18 months could go by before a tax return is filed and the election is made.

Form 1040NR is the return nonresident individuals file in the US to report their US income. While the form may look relatively easy to complete because of its brevity, it can be challenging even for an experienced tax preparer due to the many possible elections that can be made. Sample 1 shows the five pages of the most recent Form 1040NR. You can find IRS forms at apps.irs.gov/app/picklist/list/formsInstructions.html.

So how do you deal with this issue? Regardless of whether you are using a property manager or managing the property yourself, you as the owner should provide the manager or tenant

Sample 1
US Nonresident Alien Income Tax Return (Form 1040NR)

Form **1040NR**

Department of the Treasury
Internal Revenue Service

U.S. Nonresident Alien Income Tax Return

▶ Information about Form 1040NR and its separate instructions is at *www.irs.gov/form1040nr.*

For the year January 1–December 31, 2015, or other tax year
beginning , 2015, and ending , 20

OMB No. 1545-0074

20**15**

Please print or type

Your first name and initial	Last name
Present home address (number, street, and apt. no., or rural route). If you have a P.O. box, see instructions.	Check if: ☐ Individual ☐ Estate or Trust
City, town or post office, state, and ZIP code. If you have a foreign address, also complete spaces below (see instructions).	

Identifying number (see instructions)

Foreign country name	Foreign province/state/county	Foreign postal code

Filing Status

Check only one box.

1 ☐ Single resident of Canada or Mexico or single U.S. national
2 ☐ Other single nonresident alien
3 ☐ Married resident of Canada or Mexico or married U.S. national
4 ☐ Married resident of South Korea
5 ☐ Other married nonresident alien
6 ☐ Qualifying widow(er) with dependent child (see instructions)

If you checked box 3 or 4 above, enter the information below.

(i) Spouse's first name and initial	(ii) Spouse's last name	(iii) Spouse's identifying number

Exemptions

If more than four dependents, see instructions.

7a ☐ **Yourself.** If someone can claim you as a dependent, **do not** check box 7a
 b ☐ **Spouse.** Check box 7b only if you checked box 3 or 4 above **and** your spouse **did not** have any U.S. gross income

c **Dependents:** (see instructions)		(2) Dependent's identifying number	(3) Dependent's relationship to you	(4) ✔ if qualifying child for child tax credit (see instr.)
(1) First name	Last name			☐
				☐
				☐
				☐

d Total number of exemptions claimed

Boxes checked on 7a and 7b ____
No. of children on 7c who:
• lived with you ____
• did not live with you due to divorce or separation (see instructions) ____
Dependents on 7c not entered above ____
Add numbers on lines above ▶ ☐

Income Effectively Connected With U.S. Trade/ Business

Attach Form(s) W-2, 1042-S, SSA-1042S, RRB-1042S, and 8288-A here. Also attach Form(s) 1099-R if tax was withheld.

8 Wages, salaries, tips, etc. Attach Form(s) W-2		8
9a Taxable interest		9a
b Tax-exempt interest. Do not include on line 9a	9b	
10a Ordinary dividends		10a
b Qualified dividends	10b	
11 Taxable refunds, credits, or offsets of state and local income taxes (see instructions)		11
12 Scholarship and fellowship grants. Attach Form(s) 1042-S or required statement (see instructions)		12
13 Business income or (loss). Attach Schedule C or C-EZ (Form 1040)		13
14 Capital gain or (loss). Attach Schedule D (Form 1040) if required. If not required, check here ☐		14
15 Other gains or (losses). Attach Form 4797		15
16a IRA distributions	16a	16b Taxable amount (see instructions)	16b
17a Pensions and annuities	17a	17b Taxable amount (see instructions)	17b
18 Rental real estate, royalties, partnerships, trusts, etc. Attach Schedule E (Form 1040)		18
19 Farm income or (loss). Attach Schedule F (Form 1040)		19
20 Unemployment compensation		20
21 Other income. List type and amount (see instructions)		21
22 Total income exempt by a treaty from page 5, Schedule OI, Item L (1)(e)	22	
23 Combine the amounts in the far right column for lines 8 through 21. This is your **total effectively connected income** ▶		23

Adjusted Gross Income

24 Educator expenses (see instructions)	24	
25 Health savings account deduction. Attach Form 8889	25	
26 Moving expenses. Attach Form 3903	26	
27 Deductible part of self-employment tax. Attach Schedule SE (Form 1040)	27	
28 Self-employed SEP, SIMPLE, and qualified plans	28	
29 Self-employed health insurance deduction (see instructions)	29	
30 Penalty on early withdrawal of savings	30	
31 Scholarship and fellowship grants excluded	31	
32 IRA deduction (see instructions)	32	
33 Student loan interest deduction (see instructions)	33	
34 Domestic production activities deduction. Attach Form 8903	34	
35 Add lines 24 through 34		35
36 Subtract line 35 from line 23. This is your **adjusted gross income** ▶		36

For Disclosure, Privacy Act, and Paperwork Reduction Act Notice, see instructions.

Cat. No. 11364D

Form **1040NR** (2015)

Sample 1 — Continued

Tax and Credits	37 Amount from line 36 (adjusted gross income)	37
	38 **Itemized deductions** from page 3, Schedule A, line 15	38
	39 Subtract line 38 from line 37	39
	40 Exemptions (see instructions)	40
	41 **Taxable income.** Subtract line 40 from line 39. If line 40 is more than line 39, enter -0-	41
	42 **Tax** (see instructions). Check if any tax is from: **a** ☐ Form(s) 8814 **b** ☐ Form 4972	42
	43 **Alternative minimum tax** (see instructions). Attach Form 6251	43
	44 Excess advance premium tax credit repayment. Attach Form 8962	44
	45 Add lines 42, 43, and 44 . . . . ▶	45

	46 Foreign tax credit. Attach Form 1116 if required	46	
	47 Credit for child and dependent care expenses. Attach Form 2441	47	
	48 Retirement savings contributions credit. Attach Form 8880 .	48	
	49 Child tax credit. Attach Schedule 8812, if required	49	
	50 Residential energy credits. Attach Form 5695	50	
	51 Other credits from Form: **a** ☐ 3800 **b** ☐ 8801 **c** ☐	51	
	52 Add lines 46 through 51. These are your **total credits**		52
	53 Subtract line 52 from line 45. If line 52 is more than line 45, enter -0- . . . . . ▶		53

Other Taxes	54 Tax on income not effectively connected with a U.S. trade or business from page 4, Schedule NEC, line 15	54
	55 Self-employment tax. Attach Schedule SE (Form 1040)	55
	56 Unreported social security and Medicare tax from Form: **a** ☐ 4137 **b** ☐ 8919	56
	57 Additional tax on IRAs, other qualified retirement plans, etc. Attach Form 5329 if required	57
	58 Transportation tax (see instructions)	58
	59a Household employment taxes from Schedule H (Form 1040)	59a
	b First-time homebuyer credit repayment. Attach Form 5405 if required	59b
	60 Taxes from: **a** ☐ Form 8959 **b** ☐ Instructions; enter code(s)	60
	61 Add lines 53 through 60. This is your **total tax** . . . . ▶	61

Payments	62 Federal income tax withheld from:		
	a Form(s) W-2 and 1099	62a	
	b Form(s) 8805	62b	
	c Form(s) 8288-A	62c	
	d Form(s) 1042-S	62d	
	63 2015 estimated tax payments and amount applied from 2014 return	63	
	64 Additional child tax credit. Attach Schedule 8812	64	
	65 Net premium tax credit. Attach Form 8962	65	
	66 Amount paid with request for extension to file (see instructions)	66	
	67 Excess social security and tier 1 RRTA tax withheld (see instructions)	67	
	68 Credit for federal tax paid on fuels. Attach Form 4136 . .	68	
	69 Credits from Form: **a** ☐ 2439 **b** ☐ Reserved **c** ☐ 8885 **d** ☐ ____	69	
	70 Credit for amount paid with Form 1040-C	70	
	71 Add lines 62a through 70. These are your **total payments** . . . . ▶		71

Refund Direct deposit? See instructions.	72 If line 71 is more than line 61, subtract line 61 from line 71. This is the amount you **overpaid**	72
	73a Amount of line 72 you want **refunded to you.** If Form 8888 is attached, check here . ▶ ☐	73a
	b Routing number ☐☐☐☐☐☐☐☐☐ ▶ **c** Type: ☐ Checking ☐ Savings	
	d Account number ☐☐☐☐☐☐☐☐☐☐☐☐☐☐☐☐☐	
	e If you want your refund check mailed to an address outside the United States not shown on page 1, enter it here.	
	74 Amount of line 72 you want **applied to your 2016 estimated tax** ▶ 74	
Amount You Owe	75 **Amount you owe.** Subtract line 71 from line 61. For details on how to pay, see instructions ▶	75
	76 Estimated tax penalty (see instructions) 76	

Third Party Designee	Do you want to allow another person to discuss this return with the IRS (see instructions)? ☐ **Yes. Complete below.** ☐**No**
	Designee's name ▶ Phone no. ▶ Personal identification number (PIN) ▶
Sign Here Keep a copy of this return for your records.	Under penalties of perjury, I declare that I have examined this return and accompanying schedules and statements, and to the best of my knowledge and belief, they are true, correct, and complete. Declaration of preparer (other than taxpayer) is based on all information of which preparer has any knowledge.
	Your signature ▶ Date Your occupation in the United States If the IRS sent you an Identity Protection PIN, enter it here (see inst.)
Paid Preparer Use Only	Print/Type preparer's name Preparer's signature Date Check ☐ if self-employed PTIN
	Firm's name ▶ Firm's EIN ▶
	Firm's address ▶ Phone no.

Form **1040NR** (2015)

Sample 1 — Continued

Schedule A—Itemized Deductions (see instructions)

07

Taxes You Paid	1	State and local income taxes		1	
Gifts to U.S. Charities		**Caution:** If you made a gift and received a benefit in return, see instructions.			
	2	Gifts by cash or check. If you made any gift of $250 or more, see instructions	2		
	3	Other than by cash or check. If you made any gift of $250 or more, see instructions. You **must** attach Form 8283 if the amount of your deduction is over $500	3		
	4	Carryover from prior year	4		
	5	Add lines 2 through 4		5	
Casualty and Theft Losses	6	Casualty or theft loss(es). Attach Form 4684. See instructions		6	
Job Expenses and Certain Miscellaneous Deductions	7	Unreimbursed employee expenses—job travel, union dues, job education, etc. You **must** attach Form 2106 or Form 2106-EZ if required. See instructions ▶ _____	7		
	8	Tax preparation fees	8		
	9	Other expenses. See instructions for expenses to deduct here. List type and amount ▶ _____	9		
	10	Add lines 7 through 9	10		
	11	Enter the amount from Form 1040NR, line 37 . . . . . [11]			
	12	Multiply line 11 by 2% (0.02)	12		
	13	Subtract line 12 from line 10. If line 12 is more than line 10, enter -0-		13	
Other Miscellaneous Deductions	14	Other—see instructions for expenses to deduct here. List type and amount ▶ _____		14	
Total Itemized Deductions	15	Is Form 1040NR, line 37, over the amount shown below for the filing status box you checked on page 1 of Form 1040NR:			

- $309,900 if you checked box 6,
- $258,250 if you checked box 1 or 2, or
- $154,950 if you checked box 3, 4, or 5?

☐ **No.** Your deduction is not limited. Add the amounts in the far right column for lines 1 through 14. Also enter this amount on Form 1040NR, line 38.

☐ **Yes.** Your deduction may be limited. See the Itemized Deductions Worksheet in the instructions to figure the amount to enter here and on Form 1040NR, line 38.

15

Form **1040NR** (2015)

Form 1040NR (2015)

Page **4**

Schedule NEC—Tax on Income Not Effectively Connected With a U.S. Trade or Business (see instructions)

Enter amount of income under the appropriate rate of tax (see instructions)

Nature of income		(a) 10%	(b) 15%	(c) 30%	(d) Other (specify) % %
1 Dividends paid by:					
a U.S. corporations	1a				
b Foreign corporations	1b				
2 Interest:					
a Mortgage	2a				
b Paid by foreign corporations	2b				
c Other	2c				
3 Industrial royalties (patents, trademarks, etc.)	3				
4 Motion picture or T.V. copyright royalties	4				
5 Other royalties (copyrights, recording, publishing, etc.)	5				
6 Real property income and natural resources royalties	6				
7 Pensions and annuities	7				
8 Social security benefits	8				
9 Capital gain from line 18 below	9				
10 Gambling—Residents of Canada only. Enter net income in column (c).					
If zero or less, enter -0-.	10c				
a Winnings					
b Losses					
11 Gambling winnings—Residents of countries other than Canada.					
Note: Losses not allowed	11				
12 Other (specify) ▶	12				
13 Add lines 1a through 12 in columns (a) through (d)	13				
14 Multiply line 13 by rate of tax at top of each column	14				
15 Tax on income not effectively connected with a U.S. trade or business. Add columns (a) through (d) of line 14. Enter the total here and on Form 1040NR, line 54					▶ 15

Capital Gains and Losses From Sales or Exchanges of Property

16 (a) Kind of property and description (if necessary, attach statement of descriptive details not shown below)	(b) Date acquired (mo., day, yr.)	(c) Date sold (mo., day, yr.)	(d) Sales price	(e) Cost or other basis	(f) LOSS If (e) is more than (d), subtract (d) from (e)	(g) GAIN If (d) is more than (e), subtract (e) from (d)

16 Enter only the capital gains and losses from property sales or exchanges that are from sources within the United States and not effectively connected with a U.S. business. Do not include a gain or loss on disposing of a U.S. real property interest; report these gains and losses on Schedule D (Form 1040).

Report property sales or exchanges that are effectively connected with a U.S. business on Schedule D (Form 1040), Form 4797, or both.

17 Add columns (f) and (g) of line 16 17

18 Capital gain. Combine columns (f) and (g) of line 17. Enter the net gain here and on line 9 above (if a loss, enter -0-) ▶ 18

Form **1040NR** (2015)

Schedule OI—Other Information (see instructions)
Answer all questions

A Of what country or countries were you a citizen or national during the tax year? _____

B In what country did you claim residence for tax purposes during the tax year? _____

C Have you ever applied to be a green card holder (lawful permanent resident) of the United States? . . . . . . ☐ Yes ☐ No

D Were you ever:
1. A U.S. citizen? . . . . ☐ Yes ☐ No
2. A green card holder (lawful permanent resident) of the United States? . . . . ☐ Yes ☐ No
If you answer "Yes" to (1) or (2), see Pub. 519, chapter 4, for expatriation rules that apply to you.

E If you had a visa on the last day of the tax year, enter your visa type. If you did not have a visa, enter your U.S. immigration status on the last day of the tax year. _____

F Have you ever changed your visa type (nonimmigrant status) or U.S. immigration status? . . . . ☐ Yes ☐ No
If you answered "Yes," indicate the date and nature of the change. ▶ _____

G List all dates you entered and left the United States during 2015 (see instructions).
Note: If you are a resident of Canada or Mexico AND commute to work in the United States at frequent intervals,
check the box for Canada or Mexico and skip to item H . . . . ☐ Canada ☐ Mexico

Date entered United States mm/dd/yy	Date departed United States mm/dd/yy		Date entered United States mm/dd/yy	Date departed United States mm/dd/yy

H Give number of days (including vacation, nonworkdays, and partial days) you were present in the United States during:
2013 _____ , 2014 _____ , and 2015 _____ .

I Did you file a U.S. income tax return for any prior year? . . . . ☐ Yes ☐ No
If "Yes," give the latest year and form number you filed . . . ▶ _____

J Are you filing a return for a trust? . . . . ☐ Yes ☐ No
If "Yes," did the trust have a U.S. or foreign owner under the grantor trust rules, make a distribution or loan to a
U.S. person, or receive a contribution from a U.S. person? . . . . ☐ Yes ☐ No

K Did you receive total compensation of $250,000 or more during the tax year? . . . . ☐ Yes ☐ No
If "Yes," did you use an alternative method to determine the source of this compensation? . . . . ☐ Yes ☐ No

L Income Exempt from Tax—If you are claiming exemption from income tax under a U.S. income tax treaty with a foreign country, complete (1) through (3) below. See Pub. 901 for more information on tax treaties.
1. Enter the name of the country, the applicable tax treaty article, the number of months in prior years you claimed the treaty benefit, and the amount of exempt income in the columns below. Attach Form 8833 if required (see instructions).

(a) Country	**(b)** Tax treaty article	**(c)** Number of months claimed in prior tax years	**(d)** Amount of exempt income in current tax year

(e) **Total.** Enter this amount on Form 1040NR, line 22. Do not enter it on line 8 or line 12 . . . . . .
2. Were you subject to tax in a foreign country on any of the income shown in 1(d) above? . . . . ☐ Yes ☐ No
3. Are you claiming treaty benefits pursuant to a Competent Authority determination? . . . . ☐ Yes ☐ No
If "Yes," attach a copy of the Competent Authority determination letter to your return.

Form **1040NR** (2015)

with IRS Form W-8ECI (Certificate of Foreign Person's Claim That Income Is Effectively Connected With the Conduct of a Trade or Business in the United States), indicating that the income is effectively connected with a US trade or business and therefore not subject to withholding tax. See Sample 2.

Since Form W-8ECI asks for your Taxpayer Identification Number, you will need to obtain an Individual Tax Identification Number by filing Form W-7 (Application for IRS Individual Taxpayer Identification Number). The first question you are asked is "Reason you are submitting Form W-7." You will most likely want to check box "h" Other and list Exception #1(b) — Individuals who have opened an interest bearing bank deposit account that generates income that is effectively connected with their US trade or business (or rental property). See Sample 3.

Note: As an individual, there are two types of ID numbers that can be obtained; Social Security Number (SSN) or an Individual Tax Identification Number (ITIN). SSNs are only given to individuals with the legal right to work in the US, all others are issued an ITIN.

2.2 Rental income under indirect ownership

If you recall from Chapter 2, indirect ownership involves holding the property in an entity such as a corporation, partnership, or trust. The reasons someone would choose indirect ownership over direct ownership are potential asset protection, and when people other than a couple (married and common-law couples) are owners, it provides a structure and rules for operating your business. If the indirect ownership occurs through a foreign (non-US) entity, the property will most likely be considered outside of the US and not subject to US estate tax.

Caution: While more and more states are recognizing same sex marriages, the US does not generally recognize same sex marriages and does not recognize common-law marriages at all. Therefore, if you are not legally married according to US law, and you are operating a business (e.g., a rental), you will be deemed

Sample 2

Certificate of Foreign Person's Claim That Income Is Effectively Connected With the Conduct of a Trade or Business in the United States (Form W-8ECI)

Form **W-8ECI** (Rev. February 2014) Department of the Treasury Internal Revenue Service	**Certificate of Foreign Person's Claim That Income Is Effectively Connected With the Conduct of a Trade or Business in the United States** ▶ Section references are to the Internal Revenue Code. ▶ Information about Form W-8ECI and its separate instructions is at *www.irs.gov/formw8eci*. ▶ Give this form to the withholding agent or payer. Do not send to the IRS.	OMB No. 1545-1621

Note. *Persons submitting this form must file an annual U.S. income tax return to report income claimed to be effectively connected with a U.S. trade or business (see instructions).*

Do not use this form for: **Instead, use Form:**

• A beneficial owner solely claiming foreign status or treaty benefits . . . . W-8BEN or W-8BEN-E

• A foreign government, international organization, foreign central bank of issue, foreign tax-exempt organization, foreign private foundation, or government of a U.S. possession claiming the applicability of section(s) 115(2), 501(c), 892, 895, or 1443(b) W-8EXP

Note. *These entities should use Form W-8ECI if they received effectively connected income and are not eligible to claim an exemption for chapter 3 or 4 purposes on Form W-8EXP.*

• A foreign partnership or a foreign trust (unless claiming an exemption from U.S. withholding on income effectively connected with the   W-8BEN-E
  conduct of a trade or business in the United States) . . . .   or W-8IMY

• A person acting as an intermediary W-8IMY

Note. *See instructions for additional exceptions.*

Part I	**Identification of Beneficial Owner** (see instructions.)

1 Name of individual or organization that is the beneficial owner   **2** Country of incorporation or organization

3 Name of disregarded entity receiving the payments (if applicable)

4 Type of entity (check the appropriate box):   ☐ Individual   ☐ Corporation
       ☐ Partnership   ☐ Simple trust   ☐ Complex trust   ☐ Estate
       ☐ Government   ☐ Grantor trust   ☐ Central bank of issue   ☐ Tax-exempt organization
       ☐ Private foundation   ☐ International organization

5 Permanent residence address (street, apt. or suite no., or rural route). **Do not use a P.O. box or in-care-of address.**

City or town, state or province. Include postal code where appropriate.   Country

6 Business address in the United States (street, apt. or suite no., or rural route). **Do not use a P.O. box or in-care-of address.**

City or town, state, and ZIP code

7 U.S. taxpayer identification number (required—see instructions)   **8** Foreign tax identifying number
       ☐ SSN or ITIN   ☐ EIN

9 Reference number(s) (see instructions)   **10** Date of birth (MM-DD-YYYY)

11 Specify each item of income that is, or is expected to be, received from the payer that is effectively connected with the conduct of a trade or business in the United States. (attach statement if necessary) --

Part II	**Certification**

Under penalties of perjury, I declare that I have examined the information on this form and to the best of my knowledge and belief it is true, correct, and complete. I further certify under penalties of perjury that:

• I am the beneficial owner (or I am authorized to sign for the beneficial owner) of all of the payments to which this form relates,

• The amounts for which this certification is provided are effectively connected with the conduct of a trade or business in the United States,

• The income for which this form was provided is includible in my gross income (or the beneficial owner's gross income) for the taxable year, **and**

• The beneficial owner is not a U.S. person.

Furthermore, I authorize this form to be provided to any withholding agent that has control, receipt, or custody of the payments of which I am the beneficial owner or any withholding agent that can disburse or make payments of the amounts of which I am the beneficial owner.

I agree that I will submit a new form within 30 days if any certification made on this form becomes incorrect.

Sign Here

Signature of beneficial owner (or individual authorized to sign for the beneficial owner)   Print name   Date (MM-DD-YYYY)

☐ I certify that I have the capacity to sign for the person identified on line 1 of this form.

For Paperwork Reduction Act Notice, see separate instructions.   Cat. No. 25045D   Form **W-8ECI** (Rev. 2-2014)

Sample 3
Application for IRS Individual Taxpayer Identification Number (Form W-7)

Form W-7
(Rev. August 2013)
Department of the Treasury
Internal Revenue Service

Application for IRS Individual Taxpayer Identification Number

▶ For use by individuals who are not U.S. citizens or permanent residents.
▶ See instructions.

OMB No. 1545-0074

An IRS individual taxpayer identification number (ITIN) is for federal tax purposes only.

FOR IRS USE ONLY

Before you begin:

• **Do not submit** this form if you have, or are eligible to get, a U.S. social security number (SSN).

• *Getting an ITIN does not change your immigration status or your right to work in the United States and does not make you eligible for the earned income credit.*

Reason you are submitting Form W-7. Read the instructions for the box you check. **Caution:** If you check box **b, c, d, e, f,** or **g, you must file a tax return with Form W-7 unless you meet one of the exceptions** (see instructions).

a ☐ Nonresident alien required to get ITIN to claim tax treaty benefit

b ☐ Nonresident alien filing a U.S. tax return

c ☐ U.S. resident alien **(based on days present in the United States)** filing a U.S. tax return

d ☐ Dependent of U.S. citizen/resident alien } Enter name and SSN/ITIN of U.S. citizen/resident alien (see instructions) ▶ _____

e ☐ Spouse of U.S. citizen/resident alien

f ☐ Nonresident alien student, professor, or researcher filing a U.S. tax return or claiming an exception

g ☐ Dependent/spouse of a nonresident alien holding a U.S. visa

h ☐ Other (see instructions) ▶ _____

Additional information for **a** and **f**: Enter treaty country ▶ _____ and treaty article number ▶ _____

Name (see instructions)	**1a** First name	Middle name	Last name
Name at birth if different . . ▶	**1b** First name	Middle name	Last name

Applicant's mailing address

2 Street address, apartment number, or rural route number. **If you have a P.O. box, see separate instructions.**

City or town, state or province, and country. Include ZIP code or postal code where appropriate.

Foreign (non-U.S.) address (if different from above) (see instructions)

3 Street address, apartment number, or rural route number. **Do not use a P.O. box number.**

City or town, state or province, and country. Include ZIP code or postal code where appropriate.

Birth information	**4** Date of birth (month / day / year)	Country of birth	City and state or province (optional)	**5** ☐ Male ☐ Female

Other information	**6a** Country(ies) of citizenship	**6b** Foreign tax I.D. number (if any)	**6c** Type of U.S. visa (if any), number, and expiration date

6d Identification document(s) submitted (see instructions) ☐ Passport ☐ Driver's license/State I.D.
☐ USCIS documentation ☐ Other _____

Issued by: _____ No.: _____ Exp. date: / /

Date of entry into the United States (MM/DD/YYYY) / /

6e Have you previously received a Internal Revenue Service Number (IRSN) or employer identification number (EIN)?
☐ **No/Do not know.** Skip line 6f.
☐ **Yes.** Complete line 6f. If more than one, list on a sheet and attach to this form (see instructions).

6f Enter: IRSN or EIN ▶ _____ and
Name under which it was issued ▶ _____

6g Name of college/university or company (see instructions) _____
City and state _____ Length of stay _____

Sign Here

Under penalties of perjury, I (applicant/delegate/acceptance agent) declare that I have examined this application, including accompanying documentation and statements, and to the best of my knowledge and belief, it is true, correct, and complete. I authorize the IRS to disclose to my acceptance agent returns or return information necessary to resolve matters regarding the assignment of my IRS individual taxpayer identification number (ITIN), including any previously assigned taxpayer identifying number.

Signature of applicant (if delegate, see instructions) | Date (month / day / year) / / | Phone number

Keep a copy for your records.

Name of delegate, if applicable (type or print) | Delegate's relationship to applicant | ☐ Parent ☐ Court-appointed guardian ☐ Power of Attorney

Acceptance Agent's Use ONLY

Signature | Date (month / day / year) / / | Phone _____

Fax _____

Name and title (type or print) | Name of company | EIN _____ | PTIN _____

Office Code _____

For Paperwork Reduction Act Notice, see separate instructions. | Cat. No. 10229L | Form **W-7** (Rev. 8-2013)

to be operating a partnership. You should therefore consider forming a legal partnership and complying with all of the rules required of a partnership.

2.2a Rental income under a corporation

A corporation is a common way of owning real estate for Canadians, however if one of your objectives in buying US real estate is either occasional personal use, or long-term appreciation, then a corporation is not a good idea. If you plan to use the property from time to time, you must pay the corporation fair market rent or report, as a personal dividend, the value of the rent not paid. In both cases, the value of the rent will be subject to double taxation. Because of the double taxation feature of US corporations, very few people create corporations in the US any more. The reason for the double taxation is that dividends paid to shareholders are not an expense to the corporation (first level of tax) and of course the shareholder reports the dividend and pays tax on his or her individual tax return (second level of tax). The other reason to avoid corporate tax (as if double tax were not enough), is that all income is taxed at ordinary income tax rates. In other words, you miss out on the lower capital gains tax rate. Currently, the highest ordinary income tax rate is 39.6 percent, whereas the highest capital gains tax rate is 20 percent (plus state income tax, if applicable), with a few exceptions. For individuals, the current federal tax rate for long-term capital gain income can be zero percent, 15 percent, or 20 percent depending on the amount of income.

Foreign companies are subject to an additional branch profit tax imposed on the company's profit from its US business operations. The tax is up to 30 percent of after-tax profits. The Canada-US Treaty reduces the branch profits tax to 15 percent or 5 percent (if the Canadian corporation owns the property directly, the tax would be 15 percent, but if the corporation owns a US subsidiary corporation, the tax would be 5 percent. For example, if the Canadian corporation had $1,000 profit from its US operations [rental], the corporate tax would be 15 percent or $150. The after-tax profits would therefore be $850. The branch profits tax could be an additional $128 ($850 times 15 percent), assuming a 15 percent branch profits tax. The total US tax would be $278, or 27.8 percent of earnings before tax). See Table 6.

Note: In addition to regular corporate tax, a Canadian corporation may have to pay an additional "branch profits tax" of up to 15 percent (5 percent if through a US sibsidiary).

A Canadian corporation must make withholding tax payments when money is repatriated to Canada. The default withholding rate is 30 percent, but the Treaty reduces the withholding on dividends to 15 percent and 5 percent if the dividend is being paid to a Canadian parent corporation. Those payments are made using Forms 1042 (Annual Withholding Tax Return for U.S. Source Income of Foreign Persons), 1042-S (Foreign Person's U.S. Source Income Subject to Withholding) and 1042-T (Annual Summary and Transmittal of Forms 1042-S).

Table 6
Tax Tables

2016 US Individual Capital Gains Tax Table	
Income[1]	Long-term Capital Gain Rate[2]
$0 to $37,650	0 percent
$37,651 to $415,050	15 percent
$415,050+	20 percent

1 Individual income per person
2 Long-term capital gain is for property held for at least one year and one day.

2016 US Corporate Federal Tax Table	
Income	Federal Corporate Tax Rate
$0 to $50,000	15 percent
$50,001 to $75,000	25 percent
$75,001 to $100,000	34 percent
$100,001 to $335,000	39 percent
$335,001 to $10,000,000	34 percent
$10,000,001 to $15,000,000	35 percent
$15,000,001 to $18,333,333	38 percent
$18,333,334+	35 percent

2.2b Rental income under a partnership

In the US, a partnership comes in many different flavors. We have a traditional general partnership (GP), limited partnership (LP), limited liability partnership (LLP), limited liability limited partnership (LLLP) and something called a limited liability company (LLC). While an LLC is not technically a partnership, it behaves very similarly to a LLP in most cases. However, as a Canadian you should care about one difference, in particular, as it relates to how the LLC, LLP, and LLLP are treated in Canada.

In the US, a partnership is not a taxable entity, but must file a tax return to report the activity and issue a tax slip called a Schedule K-1 (Form 1065), which is a form used to report each partner's share of the income, expenses, and profits. Schedule K-1 is the document to be given to your tax preparer. All of the income, expenses, and profits flow through to the partners and the partners report the profits on their individual income tax returns; this is why a partnership is referred to as a "flow-through" entity. From a tax perspective, the individual will be required to file tax returns, the same as if the property was owned directly. See Sample 4.

An LLC is a different kind of entity; it is a hybrid that can be treated as a partnership, corporation, or sole practitioner. What determines how the LLC is treated and therefore taxed is the election that is made when the LLC is established. In the vast majority of circumstances, taxpayers elect to have the LLC taxed as a partnership. However, Canada views an LLC as a corporation, meaning that whenever a distribution from the LLC occurs, Canada will treat the distribution as a corporate dividend. So what happens is that you may have a taxable profit in LLC that you choose not to distribute because there was not enough cash or you wanted to create a reserve; this leads to taxable US income at the individual level and no Canadian tax. If, in some future year you decide that there is enough cash to make a distribution and that distribution is treated as a corporate dividend in Canada, the LLC profit (and therefore the amount that has to be reported as an individual in the US) is not likely to be as large as the distribution, since it took at least a few years to accumulate enough money to distribute.

This leads to a mismatch of foreign tax credits. The bottom line is that you would be paying taxes in both countries without the availability of foreign tax credits to offset the tax in Canada.

An example:

LLC Revenue	$12,000
Cash Expenses	$10,000
Depreciation and Amortization	$1,500
Taxable Profit*	$500
Cash in the bank	$2,000

*Referred to as net foreign business income for Canadian foreign tax credit purposes.

At the end of five years, you wound have made $2,500 in taxable profit and have $10,000 in the bank. December of the fifth year, you make an $8,000 distribution back to Canada.

Tax consequences in the US: A 10 percent tax on $500 of profit per year is $50 of income tax for years one to five, for a total of $250.

In Canada, at a 26 percent federal tax rate, there will tax of $2,080 on an $8,000 ineligible dividend, year five ($0 tax years one to four and $2,080 in year five).

In the US, there is a 30 percent withholding that will be refundable early in year six. There is no US tax owing because tax has been paid all along. For cash flow purposes, you want to move money to Canada late in the calendar year so that you can file and receive a refund as soon as possible.

2.2c Foreign tax credits

The maximum foreign Canadian tax credit a person can take (for business/rental income) in any one year is limited to the lesser of; (1) foreign income taxes paid or (2) the Canadian tax imposed on foreign income from that country. If you paid tax to more than one foreign country, you will need to perform a separate calculation for each country. The basic formula to determine eligible foreign tax credits is: net foreign business income/net income (line 236 with adjustments), times basic federal tax. If a foreign tax was paid but was not able to be used because not enough Canadian tax would be paid to absorb all of the foreign tax paid, the foreign tax can be carried forward up to three years and potentially used in the future. Unused foreign tax credits can be used for up to ten years before and three years after the current year.

Going back to our example, in years one through four there would be no tax credit because there would be no Canadian tax imposed on the US income. The $50 of US tax paid is accumulated as unused foreign tax credits, so at the end of year four there was $200 of unused foreign tax credits. In year five an additional $50 of US tax was paid and the total eligible foreign tax paid is $250. The foreign tax credit would be limited to $250 (lessor of $250 or $2,080). The ratio of net foreign business income to the net income reported on line 236 of your T1 (with adjustments). For ease of illustration, assume line 236 is $100,000. The foreign tax credit is then calculated as $500 (net foreign business income)/$100,000, times $19,407 (basic federal tax), or $97.

Because of the difference in the timing of the income and tax paid, the credit is limited to $97 rather than $250 had the income and tax been reported and paid in the same year in both countries.

Note: This example is extremely simplified for illustrative purposes. An actual calculation may have resulted in more or less credit being allowed.

A partnership that has "effectively connected taxable income" (e.g., rental income allocable to foreign partners), must make withholding tax payments. Those payments are made using Forms 8804 (Annual Return for Partnership Withholding Tax), 8805 (Foreign Partner's Information Statement), and 8813 (Partnership Withholding Tax Payment Voucher).

If a Canadian resident owns a US LLC there is no requirement to file a Canadian corporate return unless that LLC is doing business in Canada. The individual may have to file form T1135 to indicate he or she has in excess of $100,000 CAD of assets outside Canada, but would not have to report if it was personal use property. As an example, if an individual has a condo he or she is using for personal use in excess of $100,000 CAD he or she would not have to report it; if he or she were renting out the condo, it would have to be reported.

2.2d Rental income under a trust

Trusts in the US are different from those in Canada. The most common type of trust in the US is a revocable living trust. There are three features that make it unique from Canadian trusts: the trust is revocable; the trust is established by the individual for the benefit of the individual; and the trust pays no tax.

When a trust is revocable, it means that the individual can revoke it at any time. Traditionally, trusts are irrevocable, which means once established there is no turning back; this is how most trusts in Canada are formed. In general, an individual with an irrevocable trust can have no rights or control over the trust once established. The money put into the trust is considered gifted away. In the US, the revocable trust is treated as if the trust did not exist for income tax purposes, so not only does the trust pay no income tax, it does not even file a tax return. Trusts in Canada generally have a deemed disposition of the assets within the trust every 21 years. This means that the trust is deemed to dispose of and reacquire certain types of property in the trust every 21 years. The 21-year rule prevents the allocation of income and gains arising from the deemed sale, which means the entire amount (gains included) will be taxed at the top marginal tax rate.

While irrevocable trusts exist in the US, revocable trusts are more common, whereas in Canada the irrevocable trust is used. Canada does not have anything that is exactly the same as a US revocable living trust.

Sample 4
Schedule K-1 (Form 1065)

651113

☐ Final K-1   ☐ Amended K-1   OMB No. 1545-0123

Schedule K-1 (Form 1065)	20**15**

Department of the Treasury
Internal Revenue Service

For calendar year 2015, or tax
year beginning _____ , 2015
ending _____ , 20 ____

Partner's Share of Income, Deductions, Credits, etc.   ▶ See back of form and separate instructions.

Part I Information About the Partnership

A Partnership's employer identification number

B Partnership's name, address, city, state, and ZIP code

C IRS Center where partnership filed return

D ☐ Check if this is a publicly traded partnership (PTP)

Part II Information About the Partner

E Partner's identifying number

F Partner's name, address, city, state, and ZIP code

G ☐ General partner or LLC member-manager   ☐ Limited partner or other LLC member

H ☐ Domestic partner   ☐ Foreign partner

I1 What type of entity is this partner? _____
I2 If this partner is a retirement plan (IRA/SEP/Keogh/etc.), check here . . . . ☐

J Partner's share of profit, loss, and capital (see instructions):

	Beginning	Ending
Profit	%	%
Loss	%	%
Capital	%	%

K Partner's share of liabilities at year end:

Nonrecourse	. . . . . .	$ _____
Qualified nonrecourse financing	.	$ _____
Recourse	. . . . . .	$ _____

L Partner's capital account analysis:

Beginning capital account	. . .	$ _____
Capital contributed during the year		$ _____
Current year increase (decrease)	.	$ _____
Withdrawals & distributions	. .	$ (_____)
Ending capital account	. . . .	$ _____

☐ Tax basis   ☐ GAAP   ☐ Section 704(b) book
☐ Other (explain)

M Did the partner contribute property with a built-in gain or loss?
☐ Yes   ☐ No
If "Yes," attach statement (see instructions)

Part III Partner's Share of Current Year Income, Deductions, Credits, and Other Items

1	Ordinary business income (loss)	15	Credits
2	Net rental real estate income (loss)		
3	Other net rental income (loss)	16	Foreign transactions
4	Guaranteed payments		
5	Interest income		
6a	Ordinary dividends		
6b	Qualified dividends		
7	Royalties		
8	Net short-term capital gain (loss)		
9a	Net long-term capital gain (loss)	17	Alternative minimum tax (AMT) items
9b	Collectibles (28%) gain (loss)		
9c	Unrecaptured section 1250 gain		
10	Net section 1231 gain (loss)	18	Tax-exempt income and nondeductible expenses
11	Other income (loss)		
		19	Distributions
12	Section 179 deduction		
13	Other deductions	20	Other information
14	Self-employment earnings (loss)		

*See attached statement for additional information.

For IRS Use Only

For Paperwork Reduction Act Notice, see Instructions for Form 1065.   IRS.gov/form1065   Cat. No. 11394R   Schedule K-1 (Form 1065) 2015

In the US, people use revocable trusts primarily to avoid probate fees (more on those in Chapter 4). As I mentioned earlier, avoiding probate can be done in a couple of different ways that do not cost any money, so in most cases a revocable living trust is not necessary for Canadians buying real estate in the US. Few people use Canadian trusts to purchase US real estate because they have to gift the money away in order to do so.

There is one type of trust that could be beneficial in the right circumstances, and that trust is called the Cross-Border Trust. This trust is suited for second homes with a value of at least $750,000 USD. The trust provides many of the best features of US and Canadian trusts, but avoids the pitfalls.

A Cross-Border Irrevocable Trust might be a good option for people with worldwide assets greater than the US exemption amount of $5.45 million USD (2016). I will explain nonresident estate tax in more detail in Chapter 4, but in general, if a person owns US assets at death they are potentially subject to US estate tax. Because of the Treaty, every Canadian can avoid US estate tax if his or her worldwide assets are equal to or less than the exemption amount of $5.45 million USD.

Cross-Border Irrevocable Trusts are considered Canadian assets. My recommendation is to avoid trusts unless you decide a Cross-Border Irrevocable Trust is appropriate for your circumstances; corporations and partnerships are generally much better choices. For your typical investor, owning the property directly or using a US limited liability partnership are your best choices.

3. Frequently Overlooked Deductions

Some deductions frequently overlooked:

- Depreciation of land improvements (landscaping, etc.)

- Depreciation of personal property (furniture, etc.)

- First-year expensing of personal property

- Auto expenses

- Travel and entertainment

- Telephone and Internet

- Start-up and investigating expenses

- Office supplies (postage, etc.)

- Books on real estate and related topics

- Subscriptions to real estate magazines

- Tools and supplies

- Eviction costs

- Professional fees

- Tuition and registration fees for real estate courses

- Casualty or theft losses

Note: Keep track of your investigating expenses such as flights to the US, hotels, meals, consultations with lawyers and accountants, etc.; many people lose the opportunity to deduct these expenses because they do not keep track of them.

4. Taxes on Selling the Property

In the US, capital gains are broken down into short-term and long-term. A long-term gain is defined as a gain with a holding period of at least one year and a day; all other gains are defined as short-term. The reason for the distinction is that long-term gains have favorable tax treatment because the government wants to discourage short-term investing and reward longer term investing. Currently, the federal tax rate on long-term gains is a flat rate of zero percent, 15 percent, or 20 percent, with some exceptions. An additional state income tax would apply where applicable. Later in this chapter, I talk about state income taxes. Short-term gains are taxed as ordinary income, subject to the progressive tax rate system. At the lowest levels, the marginal rate is 10 percent and, at the highest, 39.6 percent.

As a nonresident alien selling real estate in the US, you will be subject to the Foreign Investment Real Property Tax Act (FIRPTA). FIRPTA states that barring an exception, the nonresident will be required to pay a 10 or 15 percent withholding tax on the gross proceeds of the real estate. The withholding would be required even if you had a loss on the sale of the property. The two most common exceptions are:

1. The buyer purchases the home for $300,000 or less and intends to occupy the property. By this, the IRS means there must be a definite plan to reside at the property at least 50 percent of the number of days the property is used by any person during the first two years. When counting the number of days the property is used, do not count the days the property is vacant.

2. The purchaser receives a statement from the seller stating that the seller is not a foreign person. This could be true if a US entity is the owner of the property.

To the extent withholding is required, the amount of withholding may be reduced below 10 percent of the gross sales price, when the IRS certifies that a reduced amount applies. Such a certification is permitted only if the seller applies to the IRS for reduced withholding by filing Form 8288-B no later than the closing date of the sale. The IRS will specify the amount of withholding required. See Sample 5.

In most cases you will want to file this form so that you are not giving an interest-free loan to the government. For example, say you bought a home for $80,000 and sold it for $100,000. Your ultimate federal tax liability will be no more than 20 percent on the $20,000 gain, or $4,000. If you do not file the form, 10 percent of $100,000, or $10,000 with be withheld, an overpayment of at least $6,000. Sure, you will receive a refund of the difference when you file your tax return, but if you sold the property in January 2015, you may not get your money back until February of 2016 at the earliest; as late as June 2016 if you filed your return in April, which is a 13–17 month interest-free loan to the government.

Sample 5
Application for Withholding Certificate for Dispositions by Foreign Persons of US Real Property Interests (Form 8288-B)

Form **8288-B** (Rev. February 2016) Department of the Treasury Internal Revenue Service	**Application for Withholding Certificate for Dispositions** **by Foreign Persons of U.S. Real Property Interests** ▶ **Please type or print.**	OMB No. 1545-1060

1 Name of transferor (attach additional sheets if more than one transferor)	Identification number

Street address, apt. or suite no., or rural route. Do not use a P.O. box.

City, state or province, and country (if not U.S.). Include ZIP code or postal code where appropriate.

2 Name of transferee (attach additional sheets if more than one transferee)	Identification number

Street address, apt. or suite no., or rural route. Do not use a P.O. box.

City, state or province, and country (if not U.S.). Include ZIP code or postal code where appropriate.

3 Applicant is: Transferor ☐   Transferee ☐

4a Name of withholding agent (see instructions)	**b** Identification number
c Name of estate, trust, or entity (if applicable)	**d** Identification number

5 Address where you want withholding certificate sent (street address, apt. or suite no., P.O. box, or rural route number)	Phone number (optional)

City, state or province, and country (if not U.S.). Include ZIP code or postal code where appropriate.

6 Description of U.S. real property transaction:

a Date of transfer (month, day, year) (see inst.) _____ **b** Contract price $ _____

c Type of interest transferred: ☐ Real property   ☐ Associated personal property
☐ Domestic U.S. real property holding corporation

d Use of property at time of sale: ☐ Rental or commercial   ☐ Personal   ☐ Other (attach explanation)

e Adjusted basis $

f Location and general description of property (for a real property interest), description (for associated personal property), or the class or type and amount of the interest (for an interest in a U.S. real property holding corporation). See instructions.

g For the 3 preceding tax years:

(1) Were U.S. income tax returns filed relating to the U.S. real property interest? . . . . ☐ Yes   ☐ No
If "Yes," when and where were those returns filed? ▶

(2) Were U.S. income taxes paid relating to the U.S. real property interest? . . . . ☐ Yes   ☐ No
If "Yes," enter the amount of tax paid for each year ▶

7 Check the box to indicate the reason a withholding certificate should be issued. See the instructions for information that must be attached to Form 8288-B.

a ☐ The transferor is exempt from U.S. tax or nonrecognition treatment applies.

b ☐ The transferor's maximum tax liability is less than the tax required to be withheld.

c ☐ The special installment sales rules described in section 7 of Rev. Proc. 2000-35 allow reduced withholding.

8 Does the transferor have any unsatisfied withholding liability under section 1445? . . . . ☐ Yes   ☐ No
See the instructions for information required to be attached.

9 Is this application for a withholding certificate made under section 1445(e)? . . . . ☐ Yes   ☐ No
If "Yes," check the applicable box in **a** and the applicable box in **b** below.

a Type of transaction: ☐ 1445(e)(1)   ☐ 1445(e)(2)   ☐ 1445(e)(3)   ☐ 1445(e)(5)   ☐ 1445(e)(6)

b Applicant is: ☐ Taxpayer   ☐ Other person required to withhold. Specify your title (e.g., trustee) ▶ _____

Under penalties of perjury, I declare that I have examined this application and accompanying attachments, and, to the best of my knowledge and belief, they are true, correct, and complete.

Signature	Title (if applicable)	Date

For Privacy Act and Paperwork Reduction Act Notice, see the instructions.   Cat. No. 10128Z   Form **8288-B** (Rev. 2-2016)

Caution: The IRS typically takes 8 weeks, but can take up to 12 weeks or more to return the withholding certificate. Send in Form 8288-B as soon as you can and when possible, make sure the closing date is far enough out to allow time for the IRS to process and return the certificate in time for the closing.

Note: FIRPTA withholding does not apply to gifts.

4.1 State income taxes

Just as in Canada, each state has the ability to tax income earned in its state. However, seven states choose not to have an income tax. Those states are Alaska, Florida, Nevada, South Dakota, Texas, Washington, and Wyoming. New Hampshire and Tennessee have nearly no income tax. Arizona has a state income tax that ranges from 2 to 4.54 percent, where the highest rate starts at $150,000 of income. California has an income tax that ranges from 1 percent to 13.3 percent, where the highest rate starts at $1,000,000.

Note: It is important to look at all of the costs of investing in one state verses another. Florida has very high personal property tax rates to make up for their lack of an income tax. They also have high insurance costs. California has both high income tax and insurance rates. Some states have a minimum tax for entities, regardless of whether you had a profit or not. California is one of those states; entities have a minimum tax of $800 per year.

4.2 Canadian filing requirements

As a Canadian resident, you are required to report your worldwide income; which of course, means that you must report your US rental income (converted to Canadian dollars) to Canada every year. In addition, you must report the value of foreign assets if in aggregate, those assets' cost basis exceeds $100,000 CAD, at any point during the year, on CRA Form T1135. Personal use real estate, e.g., a second home, and real estate used in an active business is excluded. Rented real estate does not typically rise to the level of an active business and in fact the instructions to Form

2016 State Individual Income Tax Brackets

	Single Individuals		
	Rate	as	Taxable Income
Arizona	2.59%	>	$0
	2.88%	>	$10,000
	3.36%	>	$25,000
	4.24%	>	$50,000
	4.54%	>	$150,000
California	1.00%	>	$0
	2.00%	>	$7,749
	4.00%	>	$18,371
	6.00%	>	$28,995
	8.00%	>	$40,250
	9.30%	>	$50,689
	10.30%	>	$259,844
	11.30%	>	$311,812
	12.30%	>	$519,867
	13.30%		$1,000.000

	Married Couples		
	Rate	as	Taxable Income
Arizona	2.59%	>	$0
	2.88%	>	$20,000
	3.36%	>	$50,000
	4.24%	>	$100,000
	4.54%	>	$300,000
California	1.00%	>	$0
	2.00%	>	$15,498
	4.00%	>	$36,472
	6.00%	>	$57,990
	8.00%	>	$80,500
	9.30%	>	$101,738
	10.30%	>	$519,688
	11.30%	>	$623,624
	12.30%	>	$1,000.000
	13.30%	>	$1,039,374

Table 7
Tax Filing Requirements

Situation	How It's Owned	Canadian and US Filing Requirements	Potential Canadian Forms to File	Potential US Forms to File
Second home — no rental activity	Individual or joint names	None until sold	T-1 and T1135	8288-B, W7, and 1040NR
Second home — with no/minimal rental activity	Individual or joint names	Initially	None	W7 and W-8ECI
		Annually	None	1040NR
		Upon sale	T-1 and T1135	8288-B and 1040NR
Rental property	Individual or joint names	Initially	None	W7 and W-8ECI
		Annually	T-1 and T1135	1040NR, BE-15, or BE-12C
		Upon sale	T-1 and T1135	8288-B and 1040NR
Rental property	Limited Liability Partnership or Limited Liability Limited Partnership	Initial	None	SS-4, W7, and W-8EC1
		Quarterly or Annually	T-1 and T1135	1065, 1040NR, 8804, 8805, 8813, BE-15, BE-12C, or BE-605
		Upon sale	T-1 and T1135	8288-B, 1065, and 1040NR
Rental property	Canadian Corporation and/or US Corporation	Initially	None	SS-4, W7, W-8EC1
		Quarterly or Annually	T-2 and T1134	1120, 1120F, 5471, 1042, 1042-S, BE-605
		Upon sale	T-2 and T1134	8288-B, 1120, 1120-F, 1042, 1042-S
Buy and flip	Individual or joint names	Initially	None	None
		Upon sale	T-1 and T1135	W7 and 8288-B
		Quarterly or Annually	T-1 and T1135	1040NR, BE-15, or BE-12C
Buy and flip	Limited Liability Partnership	Initially	None	SS-4 and W7
		Upon sale	T-1 and T1135	8288-B
		Quarterly or annually	T-1 and T1135	1065, 1040NR, 8804, 8805, 8813, BE-15, BE-12C, or BE-605

*Note: Application for Employer Identification Number (Form SS-4) is used when an ID number is needed for an entity. The Quarterly Survey of Foreign Direct Investment in the United States (Form BE-605) is the quarterly survey to report positions and transactions between a US company that is affiliated with a foreign parent company. Here is a guide: www.bea.gov/surveys/pdf/a-guide-to-bea-direct-investments-surveys.pdf

T1135 specifically state that rental property outside of Canada should be included.

You must provide a description of the property, country code, maximum cost amount during the year, cost amount at year end, income or loss, and the gain or loss on disposition.

Note: Don't forget to report the US bank account(s) you have opened.

If you use a Canadian corporation which owns a "foreign affiliate," (a US corporate subsidiary), and the total cost of US investments in all foreign affiliates is $100,000 CAD or more, you may be required to file Form T1134. This form is the corporate equivalent of the T1135 that individuals are required to file.

See Samples 6 and 7.

I find that a number of people are surprised to find out that they must report the rental income or capital gain when they sell a property, to both the US and Canada. If a person were to stop and think about it, it makes sense. If a person earns income in a country, the country does and should have the right to tax that income, and as a resident of Canada you are required to report and pay tax on your world income. You say, "OK, that makes sense, but doesn't that mean I will be double-taxed on the income?" No, you generally will not pay tax on the same income twice because of foreign tax credits. In general, when you pay tax in the US, that tax can be taken as a credit against your Canadian tax owed on your US income.

Example ignoring currency differences: If you have a $10,000 profit and the US taxes you $1,000 on that profit and Canada taxes you $1,500 on that same profit before credits, you are able to subtract the tax paid to the US from your gross Canadian tax, leaving you with a net $500 Canadian tax ($1,500 - $1,000 = $500). In the end, you paid $1,000 to the US and $500 to Canada, for a total of $1,500; the same tax you would have paid anyway, it is simply split between the US and Canada. Generally speaking, your total tax will always equal the tax of the highest tax country.

I am sure you have noticed that I have hedged my comment by saying "generally" a few times. The foreign tax credit mechanism is not perfect; the primary way that foreign tax credits do not work perfectly and some amount of double taxation can happen is due to timing differences. Refer to the foreign tax credit section of this chapter for additional explanation.

I find that a number of people are surprised to find out that they must report the rental income or capital gains to both the US and Canada when they sell the property. If a person were to stop and think about it, it makes sense. If a person earns income in one country, they should and do have the right to tax that income, and as a resident of Canada you are required to report and pay tax on your world income. You say, "Okay, that makes sense but doesn't that mean I will be double taxed on the income?" No, you generally will not pay tax on the same income twice because of foreign tax credits. In general, when you pay tax in the US, that tax can be taken as a credit against any Canadian tax owed on your US income.

Example ignoring currency differences: If you have a $10,000 profit and the US taxes you $1,000 on that profit and Canada taxes you $1,500 on that same profit before credits, you are able to subtract the tax paid to the US from your gross Canadian tax, leaving you with a net $500 Canadian tax ($1,500 - $1,000 = $500). In the end, you paid $1,000 to the US and $500 to Canada, for a total of $1,500; the same tax you would have paid anyway, simply split between the US and Canada. Generally speaking, your total tax will always equal the tax of the country with the highest tax.

I am sure you have noticed that I have hedged my comment by saying "generally" a few times. The foreign tax credit mechanism is not perfect; the primary way that foreign tax credits do not work perfectly and some amount of double taxation can happen is due to timing differences. Refer to section 2.2c of this chapter for additional explanation.

Sample 6
Form T1135

Canada Revenue Agency / **Agence du revenu du Canada**

For departmental use.

Foreign Income Verification Statement

- This form must be used for the 2015 and later taxation years.
- Complete and file this form if at any time in the year the total cost amount to the reporting taxpayer of all specified foreign property was more than $100,000 (Canadian).
- If an election has been made to use a functional currency (see attached instructions), state the elected functional currency code. . . . .
- See attached instructions for more information about completing this form.

If this is an amended return check this box. ☐

Identification

Check (✓) a box to indicate who you are reporting for, and complete the areas that apply

	First name	Last name	Initial	Social insurance number	Individual code
☐ Individual					☐ 1 ☐ 2

	Corporation's name		Business number (BN)	
☐ Corporation				R C

	Trust's name	Account number
☐ Trust		T – –

	Partnership's name	Partnership code	Partnership's account number	
☐ Partnership		☐ 1 ☐ 2 ☐ 3		R Z

Reporting taxpayer's address

Number   Street

City   Province or territory   Postal or zip code   Country code

For what taxation year are you filing this form?   From | Year | Month | Day | to | Year | Month | Day |

Check (✓) the appropriate box that applies for the taxation year:

☐ If the total cost of all specified foreign property held at any time during the year exceeds $100,000 but was less than $250,000, you are required to complete either Part A or Part B;

☐ If the total cost of all specified foreign property held at any time during the year was $250,000 or more, you are required to complete Part B.

Part A: Simplified reporting method

For each type of property that applies to you, check (✓) the appropriate box.

Type of property:

Funds held outside Canada . . . . ☐

Shares of non-resident corporations (other than foreign affiliates) . . . . ☐

Indebtedness owed by non-resident . . . . ☐

Interests in non-resident trusts . . . . ☐

Real property outside Canada (other than personal use and real estate used in an active business) . . . . ☐

Other property outside Canada . . . . ☐

Property held in an account with a Canadian registered securities dealer or a Canadian trust company . . . . ☐

Country code:

Select the top three countries based on the maximum cost amount of specified foreign property held during the year. Enter the country codes in the boxes below:

Income from all specified foreign property $ _____

Gain(loss) from the disposition from all specified foreign property $ _____

Privacy Act, personal information bank number CRA PPU 035

T1135 E (16)   (Ce formulaire existe en français.)

Canadá

Sample 6 — Continued

Part B: Detailed reporting method

Categories of specified foreign property

In each of the tables below, provide the required details of each specified foreign property held at any time during the particular tax year. If you need additional space, please attach a separate sheet of paper using the same format as the tables.

A taxpayer who held specified foreign property with a Canadian registered securities dealer or a Canadian trust company is permitted to report the aggregate amount, on a country-by-country basis, of all such property in Category 7, *Property held in an account with a Canadian registered securities dealer or a Canadian trust company*. See attached instructions for Category 7 for details as to how to report under this method.

1. Funds held outside Canada

Name of bank/other entity holding the funds	Country code	Maximum funds held during the year	Funds held at year end	Income
		Total		

2. Shares of non-resident corporations (other than foreign affiliates)

Name of corporation	Country code	Maximum cost amount during the year	Cost amount at year end	Income	Gain (loss) on disposition
		Total			

3. Indebtedness owed by non-resident

Description of indebtedness	Country code	Maximum cost amount during the year	Cost amount at year end	Income	Gain (loss) on disposition
		Total			

4. Interests in non-resident trusts

Name of Trust	Country code	Maximum cost amount during the year	Cost amount at year end	Income recieved	Capital received	Gain (loss) on disposition
		Total				

5. Real property outside Canada (other than personal use and real estate used in an active business)

Description of property	Country code	Maximum cost amount during the year	Cost amount at year end	Income	Gain (loss) on disposition
		Total			

6. Other property outside Canada

Description of property	Country code	Maximum cost amount during the year	Cost amount at year end	Income	Gain (loss) on disposition
		Total			

7. Property held in an account with a Canadian registered securities dealer or a Canadian trust company

Name of registered security dealer/Canadian trust company	Country code	Maximum fair market value during the year	Cost amount at year end	Income	Gain (loss) on disposition
		Total			

Privacy Act, personal information bank number CRA PPU 035

Sample 6 — Continued

Certification

I certify that the information given on this form is, to my knowledge, correct and complete, and fully discloses the reporting taxpayer's foreign property and related information.		If someone other than the taxpayer or the partnership prepared this form, provide their:	
Print name		Name	
Sign here (It is a serious offence to file a false statement.)		Address	
Position/title			
Telephone number	Date (YYYYMMDD)	Postal or zip code	Telephone number

Privacy Act, personal information bank number CRA PPU 035

Sample 7
Form T1134

Canada Revenue Agency / **Agence du revenu du Canada**

Protected B when completed

Information Return Relating to Controlled and Not-Controlled Foreign Affiliates
(2011 and later taxation years)

T1134 Summary Form

- Use this version of the return for taxation years that begin after 2010.
- This revised form T1134 is a combination of former forms T1134A and T1134B.
- Refer to the attached instructions before you complete the T1134 Summary and Supplements.
- A separate supplement must be filed for each foreign affiliate.
- Do not file a return for "dormant" or "inactive" foreign affiliates. Refer to the attached instructions for the definition of dormant or inactive foreign affiliates.
- References on this return to the foreign affiliate or the affiliate refer to the foreign affiliate for which the reporting entity is filing a supplement.
- If you are reporting on a partnership, references to year or taxation year should be read as fiscal period.
- If you need more space to report information, you can use attachments.
- If an election has been made to use functional currency (see attached instructions), state the alphabetic currency code of the functional currency. . . . .

If this is an amended return, tick this box. ☐

Do not use this area

Part I – Identification

Section 1 – Reporting entity information

Tick a box to indicate who you are reporting for, and complete the areas that apply (please print)

☐ Individual	First name	Last name		Initial	Social insurance number

☐ Corporation	Corporation's name		Business number (BN)			R C

☐ Trust	Trust's name		Account number T – –

☐ Partnership	Partnership's name		Partnership's account number		R Z

Do you have a business number for other reporting purposes (for example: GST/HST remittances, Payroll, etc.)? If so, please provide

Business number (BN)

Reporting entity's address

Number	Street

City	Province or territory	Postal code	Country code

For what taxation year are you filing this form? From [Year Month Day] To [Year Month Day]

Does this period include 2 or more short taxation years? (see attached instructions) Yes ☐ No ☐

Number of supplements attached

Section 2 – Certification

Person to contact for more information (please print)

First name	Last name	Telephone number

I, _____ (Print name), certify that the information given on these T1134 Summary and Supplements are, to the best of my knowledge, correct and complete.

Date	Authorized signing officer's, or representative's signature	Position, title, officer's rank

T1134 E (12) (Ce formulaire existe en français) Canada

Section 3 – Organizational structure

This information is required only if you are reporting on one or more "Controlled" Foreign Affiliate(s) as defined in subsection 95(1) of the Act (see attached instructions). You only have to produce the information required under this section once for a group of persons that are related to each other. If a person/partnership other than the reporting entity is filing the organizational structure, identify that person/partnership who is filing for the related group:

Name	SIN / BN / Other account number

If the following table has insufficient space, attach a separate page with a continuation of the information.

A. List the name and country code of the country of residence of each corporation (other than another foreign affiliate of the reporting entity) that is not dealing at arm's length with the reporting entity and that has an equity percentage (as defined in subsection 95(4) of the Act) in any foreign affiliate of the reporting entity. Where the reporting entity is a partnership, list the name and country code of the country of residence of each corporation that is not dealing at arm's length with the members of the partnership, and that has an equity percentage in any foreign affiliate of the reporting entity. Include the corporation's equity percentage and direct equity percentage, if any, in the foreign affiliate. (see attached instructions)

Name of related corporation	Country code of residence of corporation	Name of foreign affiliate	Country code of residence of foreign affiliate	Corporation's equity percentage in foreign affiliate	Corporation's direct equity percentage in foreign affiliate

B. List the name and country code of the country of residence of each foreign affiliate of the reporting entity that has an equity percentage in any other foreign affiliate of the reporting entity. Include the foreign affiliate's equity percentage and direct equity percentage, if any, in the other foreign affiliate.

Name of foreign affiliate	Country code of residence of foreign affiliate	Name of other foreign affiliate	Country code of residence of other foreign affiliate	Foreign affiliate's equity percentage in other foreign affiliate	Foreign affiliate's direct equity percentage in other foreign affiliate

C. If the reporting entity is a partnership, list the name, address and country code of the country of residence of each member of the partnership.

Name of partner	Address of partner	Country code of country of residence of partner

D. List the name, address and country code of the business location of each partnership of which a foreign affiliate is a member.

Partnership name	Address of partnership	Country code of country of location of partnership	Foreign affiliate	Foreign affiliate's interest percentage in the partnership

T1134 Supplement

Complete a separate supplement for each foreign affiliate and/or controlled foreign affiliate. (see attached instructions)

Part II – Foreign affiliate information

Section 1 – Reporting entity information

	Business number				Trust	Trust account number
☐ Corporation		R C		☐ Trust	T – –
☐ Partnership	Partnership account number R Z			☐ Individual	Social insurance number

		Year Month Day		Year Month Day
For what tax year are you filing this supplement?	From		To	

Section 2 – Foreign affiliate information

Where the foreign affiliate has more than one tax year ending in the reporting entity's tax year, report the required information for the second and subsequent tax year(s) of the foreign affiliate in a separate supplement.

A. Identification of foreign affiliate

Name	Address of head office

Year in which the corporation became a foreign affiliate of the reporting entity	Year	Did the corporation cease to be a foreign affiliate of the reporting entity in the year? Yes ☐ No ☐

Specify the principal activity(ies) of the foreign affiliate using the appropriate North American Industrial Classification System (NAICS) code(s). (see attached instructions for NAICS codes).

NAICS code(s) (6 digits):   1. _____   2. _____   3. _____   4. _____

Specify the countries or jurisdictions in which the foreign affiliate carries on a business or other income earning activity. Enter the appropriate country code(s). (see attached instructions for country codes).

Country code(s):   1. ____   2. ____   3. ____   4. ____

Country or jurisdiction of residence of the foreign affiliate. Enter the appropriate country code (see attached instructions).

Country code(s):   1. ____

Is this the first time that the reporting entity has filed Form T1134 for this foreign affiliate? ....   Yes ☐   No ☐

Is the foreign affiliate a controlled foreign affiliate as defined in subsection 95(1)? ....   Yes ☐   No ☐

B. Capital stock of foreign affiliate

(i) Total book cost of shares of the foreign affiliate's capital stock owned by the reporting entity as of the end of reporting entity's taxation year:

Book (historical) cost amount: _____   (state in Canadian dollars or the elected functional currency – see attached instructions)

(ii) Total book cost of shares of the foreign affiliate's capital stock at the end of reporting entity's taxation year owned by a controlled foreign affiliate of the reporting entity or other person related to the reporting entity:

Book (historical) cost amount: _____   Currency code _____

C. Other information of foreign affiliate

(i) What was the reporting entity's equity percentage in the foreign affiliate at the beginning of the reporting entity's taxation year? ....   _____ %

(ii) What was the reporting entity's equity percentage in the foreign affiliate at the end of the reporting entity's taxation year? ....   _____ %

(iii) If the Act were read without paragraph 95(2.2)(a), would the reporting entity have a qualifying interest in the foreign affiliate:

a) At the beginning of the reporting entity's taxation year? ....   Yes ☐   No ☐

b) At the end of the reporting entity's taxation year? ....   Yes ☐   No ☐

(iv) Specify the gross amount of the debt (state in Canadian dollars or the elected functional currency—see attached instructions):

a) the foreign affiliate owed to the reporting entity at the end of the reporting entity's taxation year ....   Amount _____

b) the reporting entity owed to the foreign affiliate at the end of the reporting entity's taxation year ....   Amount _____

Section 3 – Financial information of the foreign affiliate

Give the taxation year of the foreign affiliate for which the information on this return is reported: ....

	Year	Month	Day		Year	Month	Day
From				To			

For each taxation year of the foreign affiliate ending in the reporting entity's taxation year, provide the following information for the affiliate:

Attached (Tick)

- Unconsolidated financial statements (including the notes to the financial statements) or, if unavailable, the financial information that is available to you as a shareholder. ....   Yes [ ]   No [ ]

	Amount	Currency code
– Total assets	_____	[| |]
– Accounting net income before tax	_____	[| |]
– Income or profits tax paid or payable on income	_____	[| |]

- Country code to which income or profits tax was paid or payable. Enter appropriate country code(s) (see attached instructions)...............................   1. [\| \|]   2. [\| \|]   3. [\| \|]   4. [\| \|]

Section 4 – Surplus accounts

A. Surplus accounts of foreign affiliates

1. Did the reporting entity, at any time in the taxation year, receive a dividend on a share of the capital stock of the foreign affiliate? ....   Yes [ ]   No [ ]

If **yes**, provide the amount of dividend (stated in Canadian dollars or the elected functional currency) and from which surplus account:

Amount	_____	Exempt surplus	Amount	_____	Taxable surplus
Amount	_____	Pre-acquisition surplus	Amount	_____	Hybrid surplus

If **yes**, and the reporting entity is a corporation, the reporting entity must maintain summary calculations of the exempt surplus, exempt deficit, taxable surplus, taxable deficit, hybrid surplus, hybrid deficit, and underlying foreign tax of the foreign affiliate at the end of the affiliate's last taxation year ending in the reporting entity's taxation year in support of the dividend deduction claimed. Documentation supporting these calculations need not be filed but should be retained as it may be requested for examination. Surplus calculations should be made in the calculating currency under subsection 5907(6) of the *Income Tax Regulations*.

2. Was a subsection 93(1) election made or will such an election be made for the disposition of shares of the foreign affiliate in the year? ....   Yes [ ]   No [ ]

If **yes**, provide the actual or estimated amount elected on: _____   Currency code [\| \|]

B. Surplus accounts and share transactions of controlled foreign affiliates (for not-controlled foreign affiliates, only complete "A" above and go to Part IV)

1. At any time in the taxation year of the reporting entity, was the reporting entity or any foreign affiliate of the reporting entity involved in a corporate or other organization, reorganization, amalgamation, merger, winding-up, liquidation, dissolution, division, or an issuance, redemption, or cancellation of share capital or a similar transaction in a manner that affected the exempt surplus, exempt deficit, taxable surplus, taxable deficit, hybrid surplus, hybrid deficit, or underlying foreign tax of the affiliate for the reporting entity?...   Yes [ ]   No [ ]

If the answer is **yes**, provide a summary description of each transaction or event.

2. At any time in the taxation year of the reporting entity, did the reporting entity or another foreign affiliate of the reporting entity acquire or dispose of a share of the capital stock of the foreign affiliate?...   Yes [ ]   No [ ]

If the answer is **yes**, provide a summary description of each transaction or event.

Part III – Nature of income of "controlled" foreign affiliate (do not complete for not-controlled foreign affiliates)

Section 1 – Employees per business

How many full-time employees or employee equivalents (as defined in subparagraphs (c)(i) and (ii) of the **investment business** definition in subsection 95(1) of the Act) did the foreign affiliate employ on a business by business basis throughout each taxation year of the affiliate ending in the reporting entity's taxation year? (Enter the appropriate NAICS code(s) from the link in the attached instructions).

| | Business (NAICS) code | Number of full-time employees or employee equivalents | | | Business (NAICS) code | Number of full-time employees or employee equivalents | |
		1 to 5	More than 5			1 to 5	More than 5
1.		☐	☐	3.		☐	☐
2.		☐	☐	4.		☐	☐

Section 2 – Composition of revenue

Give the amount of the controlled foreign affiliate's gross revenue from a business or property for the affiliate's taxation year(s) ending in the reporting entity's taxation year, derived from each of the following sources:

Source	Foreign affiliate's gross revenue amount and currency code	
(i) Interest – From other foreign affiliates of the reporting entity	Amount	Currency code
Interest – Other	Amount	Currency code
(ii) Dividends – From other foreign affiliates of the reporting entity	Amount	Currency code
Dividends – Other	Amount	Currency code
(iii) Royalties	Amount	Currency code
(iv) Rental and leasing activities	Amount	Currency code
(v) Loans or lending activities	Amount	Currency code
(vi) Insurance or reinsurance of risks	Amount	Currency code
(vii) Factoring of trade accounts receivable	Amount	Currency code
(viii) Disposition of investment property	Amount	Currency code

Section 3 – Foreign accrual property income (FAPI)

(i) Did the foreign affiliate earn FAPI in any taxation year of the affiliate that ended in the reporting entity's taxation year?		Yes ☐ No ☐
(ii) If yes, give the reporting entity's total participating percentage for the foreign affiliate for that year.		%
Also, give the gross amount of FAPI the affiliate earned that year in respect of each of the following:		**Amount**
(i) FAPI that is income from property under subsection 95(1) of the Act		
(ii) FAPI from the sale of property under paragraph 95(2)(a.1) of the Act		
(iii) FAPI from the insurance or reinsurance of risks under paragraph 95(2)(a.2) of the Act		
(iv) FAPI from indebtedness and lease obligations under paragraph 95(2)(a.3) of the Act		
(v) FAPI from indebtedness and lease obligations under paragraph 95(2)(a.4) of the Act		
(vi) FAPI from providing services under paragraph 95(2)(b) of the Act		
(vii) FAPI from the disposition of capital property		
(viii) FAPI under the description of C in the definition of FAPI in subsection 95(1) of the Act		
	Total	0

Section 4 – Capital gains and losses

(i) Excluded property

Did the foreign affiliate dispose of a share in another foreign affiliate that was excluded property or an interest in a partnership that was excluded property in a taxation year of the affiliate that ended in the reporting entity's taxation year?...... Yes ☐ No ☐

(ii) Property that is not excluded property

Did the foreign affiliate dispose of capital property that was not excluded property in a taxation year of the affiliate that ended in the reporting entity's taxation year?...... Yes ☐ No ☐

Sample 7 — Continued

Section 5 – Income included in income from an active business

Was income of the foreign affiliate that would otherwise have been included in its income from property included in its income from an active business? If **yes**, please specify which of the below apply by ticking the appropriate "yes" or "no" box.

	Yes	No
because of subparagraph 95(2)(a)(i) of the Act?	☐	☐
because of subparagraph 95(2)(a)(ii) of the Act?	☐	☐
because of subparagraph 95(2)(a)(iii) of the Act?	☐	☐
because of subparagraph 95(2)(a)(iv) of the Act?	☐	☐
because of subparagraph 95(2)(a)(v) of the Act?	☐	☐
because of subparagraph 95(2)(a)(vi) of the Act?	☐	☐
because of the type of business carried on and the number of persons employed by the foreign affiliate in the business pursuant to paragraphs (a) and (b) of the definition of investment business in subsection 95(1) of the Act?	☐	☐
because of paragraph 95(2)(l) of the Act?	☐	☐

Was income of the foreign affiliate that would otherwise have been included in its income from a business other than an active business included in its income from an active business? If **yes**, please specify which of the below apply by ticking the appropriate "yes" or "no" box.

	Yes	No
because of the 90% test in paragraphs 95(2)(a.1) through (a.4) of the Act?	☐	☐
because of subsection 95(2.3) of the Act?	☐	☐
because of subsection 95(2.4) of the Act?	☐	☐

Part IV – Disclosure (To be completed for both not-controlled foreign affiliates and controlled foreign affiliates)

Is any information requested in this return not available?.. Yes ☐ No ☐

If **yes**, please specify below

4

Nonresident US Estate Tax and Probate

Unlike Canada, which taxes any previously untaxed income at death, the US system taxes the value of your assets at death. As you might imagine, Canadians have a lot of misinformation about US estate tax. Canadians hear stories about a 40 percent tax levied on a person's net worth and are horrified. If the estate tax system actually worked like that, there would be reason for surprise, but fortunately important bits of information are missing from this explanation.

In 2015, the US estate tax system provided American citizens and American residents with an exemption of $5.43 million in assets per person. Approximately 2.5 million Americans die each year and only about 1 in 750 deaths results in a taxable estate; 99.87 percent of deaths triggered no estate tax.[1]

As far as I can tell, there is no data on the number of Canadian residents with assets in the US that pay the US nonresident estate tax. I imagine the number is very small, or at least it should be.

1 "Table T09-0400," Taxpolicycenter.org, accessed July, 2015.

We occasionally find a case in which a Canadian has passed away and his or her estate has paid US estate tax unnecessarily because his or her advisors did not know that the US-Canada Tax Convention (Treaty) provided complete relief in most situations.

1. Green Card Holders

The taxation of green card holders would normally be outside the scope of this book, but because of its importance as well as the amount of confusion surrounding the tax status of green card holders, I will address the issue in some detail.

The most confusing aspect of being a green card holder is that immigration and tax laws are not congruent. For *immigration purposes*, a person's status as a *lawful permanent resident* will generally be abandoned after the person has been out of the US for more than six months without permission. The United States Citizenship and Immigration Service (USCIS) will not rule on a person's status until he or she attempts to return to the US claiming to be a permanent resident.

For *tax purposes*, a person is treated as a lawful permanent resident until there has been a formal determination that his or her status has been abandoned. Support for this claim can be found in the Joint Committee on Taxation's "General Explanation of the Revenue Provisions of the Deficit Reduction Act of 1984," which states:

The Act defines "lawful permanent resident" to mean an individual who has the status of having been lawfully accorded the privilege of residing permanently in the United States as an immigrant in accordance with the immigration laws, if such has not been revoked or administratively or judicially determined to have been abandoned. Therefore, an alien who comes to the United States so infrequently that, on scrutiny, he or she is no longer legally entitled to permanent resident status, will be a resident for tax purposes. The purpose for this requirement of revocation or determination is to prevent aliens from attempting to retain an apparent right to enter or remain in the United States while attempting to avoid the tax responsibility that accompanies that right.

The way for a green card holder to give notice of termination of residency is by completing Record of Abandonment of Lawful Permanent Resident Status (Form I-407) in the presence of a diplomatic or consular officer, or at a port of entry of the US in the presence of an immigration official.

In summary, unless you have formally terminated your permanent residence status by properly filing Form I-407, you continue to be a resident for tax purposes and must file US returns on your worldwide income and your heirs must file an estate tax return at your death.

The remainder of this chapter will explain how the US estate tax works for nonresidents and how the Treaty can provide relief.

2. As a Nonresident, When Are You Subject to US Estate Tax?

A nonresident of the US is subject to estate tax on only those assets that are situated in the US at the time of his or her death. The term "asset" has a broad meaning and includes all property, real or personal, tangible or intangible. An example of real property would be land and any buildings on that land. Examples of personal property would be all of the things in the building and would include vehicles. A tangible asset is something you can hold, such as gold and collectibles, whereas intangible assets are things you cannot hold directly such as corporations and other financial instruments.

The nonresident estate tax does not apply to US citizens and green card holders resident in Canada (or any other foreign country). US citizens and green card holders are subject to US estate tax on their worldwide assets, regardless of where they were living when they died.

Note: Canadian residents that are *neither* US citizens nor US green card holders are subject to tax on only their US assets at the time of their death. Canadian residents that are *either* US citizens or US green card holders are subject to tax on their worldwide assets, wherever located, at the time of their death.

Not all assets situated in the US are included in the estate of a nonresident, because certain assets are exempt from nonresident estate tax. The most common of these assets include the following:

- US bank accounts not used in connection with a trade or business (e.g., checking, savings, certificate of deposit, and bank money market accounts). Money market mutual funds are not bank accounts and are not exempt. Basically, if it is covered by Federal Deposit Insurance Corporation (FDIC) insurance, it is exempt

- Life insurance issued by a US insurer and insurance proceeds

- Certain debt obligations

- American depository receipts (ADR)

- US assets that are held in a foreign entity such as a corporation

Note: Assets may be subject to probate even if exempt from estate tax. Probate is discussed in section 4.

Any asset that is not exempt must be included in the nonresident estate. Some assets that may not be obvious to you include:

- House furnishings

- Vehicles that are licensed and kept in the US

- Golf club memberships

- US pensions, if there is a survivor benefit

Nonrecourse debt is a subtraction from your assets in determining your taxable estate. Nonrecourse debt is a loan that has only the property as collateral. In other words, the lender cannot go after other assets to collect on the loan if you do not or cannot pay. Not all debt can be subtracted in determining your taxable estate, only nonrecourse debt.

The US Internal Revenue Code allows an exemption of $60,000 of taxable assets per person. However, the US-Canada Tax Treaty allows for a greater exemption if you are willing to disclose your worldwide assets. Article XXIX B (Death Taxes) is reproduced below along with my comments in italics.

2.1 The US-Canada Tax Convention (Treaty) Article XXIX B (Taxes Imposed by Reason of Death)

1. Where the property of an individual who is a resident of a Contracting State passes by reason of the individual's death to an organization referred to in paragraph 1 of Article XXI (Exempt Organizations), and that is a resident of the other Contracting State —

    (a) If the individual is a resident of the United States and the organization is a resident of Canada, the tax consequences in the United States arising out of the passing of the property shall apply as if the organization were a resident of the United States; and

    (b) If the individual is a resident of Canada and the organization is a resident of the United States, the tax consequences in Canada arising out of the passing of the property shall apply as if the individual had disposed of the property for proceeds equal to an amount elected on behalf of the individual for this purpose (in a manner specified by the competent authority of Canada), which amount shall be no less than the individual's cost of the property as determined for purposes of Canadian tax and no greater than the fair market value of the property.

This provision allows Canadians who are neither US citizens nor green card holders a deduction for US estate tax purposes if the charitable bequest is made to a US charity. An estate deduction will also be allowed for a bequest to a Canadian charity to the extent the asset donated was subject to US estate tax.

2. In determining the estate tax imposed by the United States, the estate of an individual (other than a citizen of the United States or green card holder) who was a resident of Canada at the time of the individual's death shall be allowed a unified credit equal to the greater of —

   (a)   The amount that bears the same ratio to the credit allowed under the law of the United States to the estate of a citizen of the United States as the value of the part of the individual's gross estate that at the time of the individual's death is situated in the United States bears to the value of the individual's entire gross estate wherever situated; and

The unified credit is a tax credit that is allowed on the assets that are exempted from tax. For example, a nonresident is allowed a $60,000 exemption by law, not considering the Treaty. The estate tax on $60,000 is $13,000. The basic unified credit is therefore $13,000, which is the same thing as saying that $60,000 of assets are exempt from tax. The exemption in 2015 was $5,430,000 per person. The unified credit for that amount is $2,117,800. This section says that a Canadian resident is allowed an exemption from US estate tax equal to the ratio of US assets to worldwide assets.

Example: If you purchase a home in the US for $200,000 and your worldwide assets are $1,000,000, your ratio is 20 percent. You then apply the 20 percent to the unified credit amount of $5,430,000 (2015). This gives you $1,086,000 of tax you can avoid. See section 2.2 for more information.

   (b)   The unified credit allowed to the estate of a nonresident not a citizen of the United States under the law of the United States.

      The amount of any unified credit otherwise allowable under this paragraph shall be reduced by the amount of any credit previously allowed with respect to any gift made by the individual. A credit otherwise allowable under subparagraph (a) shall be allowed only if all information necessary for the verification and computation of the credit is provided.

There are two caveats to paragraph (b). The first one is that you must reduce the credit (exemption) by the amount of credit (exemption) previously taken under the US gift tax rules. The second caveat is that you must file the US Gift Tax Return (Form 709-NA) and provide proof of the computation. Primarily the IRS is after proof of the denominator (worldwide assets).

Caution: When calculating the credit, use the percentage of the credit allowed for Americans, not the tax owing on the assets resulting in applying the percentage to the asset equivalent.

It makes sense that the IRS would want you to file and report your worldwide assets, given that it is giving you a higher exemption based on those worldwide assets. The IRS would want to make sure the number is accurate. If you do not want to report worldwide assets to the IRS, you have the option of not using the Treaty benefit, and using the $60,000 exemption that would be allowed. The downside to this is that you almost certainly would have to pay US estate taxes.

Note: Nonresidents are subject to gift tax on gifts of assets located in the US. If you gift your US property to your children, you must file a gift tax return, Form 709. In 2015, the IRS allows an annual gift tax exclusion of up to $14,000 per person, per year. If held jointly, each can gift up to $14,000, per person, per year. That means that if a couple has two children they would like to gift a US condo to, they can gift up to $28,000 per child, or $56,000 per year. Gifts in excess of the annual exclusion will reduce their estate tax exclusion. For example, if a couple were to gift their $200,000 condo to their two children, the couple will be required to file gift tax returns and reduce the estate tax exclusion amount by $72,000 each. The gift of a $200,000 condo owned jointly is a gift of $100,000 each. Each owner can gift $28,000 per person ($14,000 times two children), meaning there was a "taxable gift" of $72,000.

3. In determining the estate tax imposed by the United States on an individual's estate with respect to property that passes to the surviving spouse of the individual (within the meaning of the law of the United States) and that would qualify for the estate tax marital deduction under the law of the United States if the surviving spouse were

a citizen of the United States and all applicable elections were properly made (in this paragraph and paragraph 4 referred to as "qualifying property"), a nonrefundable credit computed in accordance with the provisions of paragraph 4 shall be allowed in addition to the unified credit allowed to the estate under paragraph 2 or under the law of the United States, provided that —

(a) The individual was at the time of death a citizen of the United States or a resident of either Contracting State;

(b) The surviving spouse was at the time of the individual's death a resident of either Contracting State;

(c) If both the individual and the surviving spouse were residents of the United States at the time of the individual's death, one or both was a citizen of Canada; and

(d) The executor of the decedent's estate elects the benefits of this paragraph and waives irrevocably the benefits of any estate tax marital deduction that would be allowed under the law of the United States on a United States Federal estate tax return filed for the individual's estate by the date on which a qualified domestic trust election could be made under the law of the United States.

US citizens are allowed to pass assets to their surviving spouses at death without estate tax. Except for the benefits of the Treaty, noncitizen spouses are not allowed to receive unlimited amounts of assets to be passed to them by their deceased spouse. This provision eases the impact of that law through a marital credit. The credit is calculated in paragraph 4.

4. The amount of the credit allowed under paragraph 3 shall equal the lesser of —

(a) The unified credit allowed under paragraph 2 or under the law of the United States (determined without regard to any credit allowed previously with respect to any gift made by the individual), and

(b) The amount of estate tax that would otherwise be imposed by the United States on the transfer of qualifying property.

The amount of estate tax that would otherwise be imposed by the United States on the transfer of qualifying property shall equal the amount by which the estate tax (before allowable credits) that would be imposed by the United States if the qualifying property were included in computing the taxable estate exceeds the estate tax (before allowable credits) that would be so imposed if the qualifying property were not so included. Solely for purposes of determining other credits allowed under the law of the United States, the credit provided under paragraph 3 shall be allowed after such other credits.

This paragraph allows up to double the credit when property is passing to a surviving spouse.

5. Where an individual was a resident of the United States immediately before the individual's death, for the purposes of subsections 70(5.2) and (6) of the *Income Tax Act*, both the individual and the individual's spouse shall be deemed to have been resident in Canada immediately before the individual's death. Where a trust that would be a trust described in subsection 70(6) of that Act, if its trustees that were residents or citizens of the United States or domestic corporations under the law of the United States were residents of Canada, requests the competent authority of Canada to do so, the competent authority may agree, subject to terms and conditions satisfactory to such competent authority, to treat the trust for the purposes of that Act as being resident in Canada for such time as may be stipulated in the agreement.

This paragraph is generally not applicable to residents of Canada.

6. In determining the amount of Canadian tax payable by an individual who immediately before death was a resident of Canada, or by a trust described in subsection 70(6) of the *Income Tax Act* (or a trust which is treated as being resident in Canada under the provisions of paragraph 5), the amount of any Federal or state estate or inheritance taxes payable in the United States (not exceeding, where the individual was a citizen of the United States or a former citizen referred to in paragraph 2 of Article XXIX (Miscellaneous Rules), the amount of estate and inheritance taxes that would have been payable if the individual were not a citizen or former citizen of the United States) in respect of property situated within the United States shall —

   (a) To the extent that such estate or inheritance taxes are imposed upon the individual's death, be allowed as a deduction from the amount of any Canadian tax otherwise payable by the individual for the taxation year in which the individual died on the total of —

      (i) Any income, profits, or gains of the individual arising [within the meaning of paragraph 3 of Article XXIV (Elimination of Double Taxation)] in the United States in that year; and

      (ii) Where the value, at the individual's death, of the individual's entire gross estate wherever situated (determined under the law of the United States) exceeded 1.2 million US dollars or its equivalent in Canadian dollars, any income, profits, or gains of the individual for that year from property situated in the United States at that time; and

   (b) To the extent that such estate or inheritance taxes are imposed upon the death of the individual's surviving spouse, be allowed as a deduction from the amount of any Canadian tax otherwise payable by the trust for its taxation year in which that spouse dies on any income, profits, or gains of the trust for that year arising [within the meaning of paragraph 3 of Article XXIV (Elimination of Double Taxation)] in the United States or from property situated in the United States at the time of death of the spouse.

For purposes of this paragraph, property shall be treated as situated within the United States if it is so treated for estate tax purposes under the law of the United States as in effect on *March 17, 1995*, subject to any subsequent changes thereof that the competent authorities of the Contracting States have agreed to apply for the purposes of this paragraph. The deduction allowed under this paragraph shall take into account the deduction for any income tax paid or accrued to the United States that is provided under paragraph 2(a), 4(a) or 5(b) of Article XXIV (Elimination of Double Taxation).

This paragraph sets out the calculation of Canadian income taxes payable by a resident of Canada due to death. It also allows for a credit of US estate tax paid.

Important: *The Treaty allows for a tax credit for estate taxes paid in the US on the Canadian decedent's final income tax return. This means that even if US estate tax is paid, it would typically have little to no effect on the overall death taxes paid.*

7. In determining the amount of estate tax imposed by the United States on the estate of an individual who was a resident or citizen of the United States at the time of death, or upon the death of a surviving spouse with respect to a qualified domestic trust created by such an individual or the individual's executor or surviving spouse, a credit shall be allowed against such tax imposed in respect of property situated outside the United States, for the federal and provincial income taxes payable in Canada in respect of such property by reason of the death of the individual or, in the case of a qualified domestic trust, the individual's surviving spouse. Such credit shall be computed in accordance with the following rules:

(a) A credit otherwise allowable under this paragraph shall be allowed regardless of whether the identity of the taxpayer under the law of Canada corresponds to that under the law of the United States.

(b) The amount of a credit allowed under this paragraph shall be computed in accordance with the provisions and subject to the limitations of the law of the United States regarding credit for foreign death taxes (as it may be amended from time to time without changing the general principle hereof), as though the income tax imposed by Canada were a creditable tax under that law.

(c) A credit may be claimed under this paragraph for an amount of federal or provincial income tax payable in Canada only to the extent that no credit or deduction is claimed for such amount in determining any other tax imposed by the United States, other than the estate tax imposed on property in a qualified domestic trust upon the death of the surviving spouse.

This paragraph allows for a credit of Canadian federal and provincial taxes paid, on the US estate tax return.

8. Provided that the value, at the time of death, of the entire gross estate wherever situated of an individual who was a resident of Canada (other than a citizen of the United States) at the time of death does not exceed 1.2 million U.S. dollars or its equivalent in Canadian dollars, the United States may impose its estate tax upon property forming part of the estate of the individual only if any gain derived by the individual from the alienation of such property would have been subject to income taxation by the United States in accordance with Article XIII (Gains).

This paragraph provides an exemption of US estate tax for residents of Canada with estates of $1.2 million USD or less (increased in 2016 to $5,450,000 USD).

2.2 How the US nonresident estate tax works

As a Canadian resident, you are allowed an exemption equal to the pro-rata amount an American is allowed. The ratio is based on your US assets over your worldwide assets. That ratio is then applied to the exemption to arrive at an exemption amount.

> **Example 1**: Margret purchased a home in the US one year ago at a price of $120,000. She furnished the house for $40,000. Margret died when the property had a fair market value (FMV) of $125,000. The furnishings had an FMV of $25,000.
>
> Margret's US estate, when she died, was valued at $150,000 ($125,000 for the house and $25,000 for furnishing). Note that the value of the furnishing declined from $40,000 to $25,000 based on FMV at the date of death. Margret's worldwide estate was valued at $5,000,000. This resulted in 3 percent of her assets being located in the US and this percentage was applied to credit of $2,125,800 (tax on $5,450,000 of assets), resulting in an available credit of $63,774. There was $2,500 of US administrative expenses associated with the death. See Sample 8.

Note: Even though the credit available is $63,774, and the tax before the credit is only $38,778, the credit is therefore limited to the amount of the tax otherwise owing. This type of credit cannot generate a refund; it is limited to lesser of the credit amount or the gross estate tax.

When calculating the credit, use the percentage of the exemption allowed to Americans ($2,125,800). Do not apply the percentage to your US assets ($5,450,000), and then calculate the estate tax on that number. Advisors occasionally take shortcuts when describing to clients how the Treaty works and this is one of those shortcuts that can lead to mistakes.

Caution: Just because there will be no estate tax due does not mean that you do not have to file an estate tax return. You must file Form 706-NA to prove the denominator (i.e., your worldwide assets). Remember, if you do not want to disclose

Sample 8
United States Estate (and Generation-Skipping Transfer) Tax Return (Form 706-NA) (Example 1)

Form **706-NA**	United States Estate (and Generation-Skipping Transfer) Tax Return	
(Rev. August 2013)	Estate of nonresident not a citizen of the United States	OMB No. 1545-0531
Department of the Treasury Internal Revenue Service	To be filed for decedents dying after December 31, 2011. ▶ Information about Form 706-NA and its separate instructions is at *www.irs.gov/form706na*.	

Attach supplemental documents and translations. Show amounts in U.S. dollars.

Part I — Decedent, Executor, and Attorney

1a Decedent's first (given) name and middle initial		**b** Decedent's last (family) name	2 U.S. taxpayer ID number (if any)
Margret		Money	123-45-6789

3 Place of death	4 Domicile at time of death	5 Citizenship (nationality)	6 Date of death
Canada	Canada	Canadian	01/01/2016

7a Date of birth	**b** Place of birth	8 Business or occupation
01/01/1938	Canada	Retired

	9a Name of executor	10a Name of attorney for estate
In United States	**b** Address	**b** Address
	11a Name of executor	12a Name of attorney for estate
Outside United States	**b** Address (City or town, state or province, country, and ZIP or foreign postal code.)	**b** Address (City or town, state or province, country, and ZIP or foreign postal code.)

Part II — Tax Computation

1	Taxable estate from Schedule B, line 9	1	149,925
2	Total taxable gifts of tangible or intangible property located in the U.S., transferred (directly or indirectly) by the decedent after December 31, 1976, and not included in the gross estate (see section 2511)	2	0
3	Total. Add lines 1 and 2	3	149.925
4	Tentative tax on the amount on line 3 (see instructions)	4	38,778
5	Tentative tax on the amount on line 2 (see instructions)	5	0
6	Gross estate tax. Subtract line 5 from line 4	6	38,778
7	Unified credit. Enter smaller of line 6 amount or maximum allowed (see instructions)	7	38,778
8	Balance. Subtract line 7 from line 6	8	0
9	Other credits (see instructions) 9 0		
10	Credit for tax on prior transfers. Attach Schedule Q, Form 706 . . . . 10 0		
11	Total. Add lines 9 and 10	11	0
12	Net estate tax. Subtract line 11 from line 8	12	0
13	Total generation-skipping transfer tax. Attach Schedule R, Form 706	13	0
14	**Total transfer taxes.** Add lines 12 and 13	14	0
15	Earlier payments. See instructions and attach explanation	15	0
16	Balance due. Subtract line 15 from line 14 (see instructions)	16	0

Under penalties of perjury, I declare that I have examined this return, including accompanying schedules and statements, and to the best of my knowledge and belief, it is true, correct, and complete. I understand that a complete return requires listing all property constituting the part of the decedent's gross estate (as defined by the statute) situated in the United States. Declaration of preparer other than the executor is based on all information of which preparer has any knowledge.

Sign Here

▶ _____ Signature of executor   ▶ _____ Date

▶ _____ Signature of executor   ▶ _____ Date

Paid Preparer Use Only	Print/Type preparer's name	Preparer's signature	Date	Check ☐ if self-employed	PTIN
	Firm's name ▶			Firm's EIN ▶	
	Firm's address ▶			Phone no.	

For Privacy Act and Paperwork Reduction Act Notice, see the separate instructions.   Cat. No. 10145K   Form **706-NA** (Rev. 8-2013)

Form 706-NA (Rev. 8-2013)   Page **2**

Part III **General Information**

		Yes	No
1a	Did the decedent die testate?		✓
b	Were letters testamentary or of administration granted for the estate?		✓
	If granted to persons other than those filing the return, include names and addresses on page 1.		
2	Did the decedent, at the time of death, own any:		
a	Real property located in the United States?	✓	
b	U.S. corporate stock?		✓
c	Debt obligations of (1) a U.S. person, or (2) the United States, a state or any political subdivision, or the District of Columbia?		✓
d	Other property located in the United States?	✓	
3	Was the decedent engaged in business in the United States at the date of death?		✓
4	At the date of death, did the decedent have access, personally or through an agent, to a safe deposit box located in the United States?		✓
5	At the date of death, did the decedent own any property located in the United States as a joint tenant with right of survivorship; as a tenant by the entirety; or, with surviving spouse, as community property?	✓	
	If "Yes," attach Schedule E, Form 706.		
6a	Had the decedent ever been a citizen or resident of the United States (see instructions)?		✓
b	If "Yes," did the decedent lose U.S. citizenship or residency within 10 years of death? (see instructions)		✓

		Yes	No
7	Did the decedent make any transfer (of property that was located in the United States at either the time of the transfer or the time of death) described in sections 2035, 2036, 2037, or 2038 (see the instructions for Form 706, Schedule G)?		✓
	If "Yes," attach Schedule G, Form 706.		
8	At the date of death, were there any trusts in existence that were created by the decedent and that included property located in the United States either when the trust was created or when the decedent died?		✓
	If "Yes," attach Schedule G, Form 706.		
9	At the date of death, did the decedent:		
a	Have a general power of appointment over any property located in the United States?		✓
b	Or, at any time, exercise or release the power?		✓
	If "Yes" to either a or b, attach Schedule H, Form 706.		
10a	Have federal gift tax returns ever been filed?		✓
b	Periods covered ▶		
c	IRS offices where filed ▶		
11	Does the gross estate in the United States include any interests in property transferred to a "skip person" as defined in the instructions to Schedule R of Form 706?		✓
	If "Yes," attach Schedules R and/or R-1, Form 706.		

Schedule A. Gross Estate in the United States (see instructions)

	Yes	No
Do you elect to value the decedent's gross estate at a date or dates after the decedent's death (as authorized by section 2032)? ▶		✓

*To make the election, you must check this box "Yes." If you check "Yes," complete **all** columns. If you check "No," complete columns (a), (b), and (e); you may leave columns (c) and (d) blank or you may use them to expand your column (b) description.*

(a) Item no.	(b) Description of property and securities For securities, give CUSIP number	(c) Alternate valuation date	(d) Alternate value in U.S. dollars	(e) Value at date of death in U.S. dollars
1	Single family home at 123 State Street, Anywhere USA	N/A	N/A	125,000
2	Furnishings at 123 State Street, Anywhere USA	N/A	N/A	25,000
	(If you need more space, attach additional sheets of same size.)			
Total			N/A	150,000

Schedule B. Taxable Estate

Caution. You must document lines 2 and 4 for the deduction on line 5 to be allowed.

1	Gross estate in the United States (Schedule A total)	**1**	150,000
2	Gross estate outside the United States (see instructions)	**2**	4,850,000
3	Entire gross estate wherever located. Add amounts on lines 1 and 2	**3**	5,000,000
4	Amount of funeral expenses, administration expenses, decedent's debts, mortgages and liens, and losses during administration. Attach itemized schedule. (see instructions)	**4**	2,500
5	Deduction for expenses, claims, etc. Divide line 1 by line 3 and multiply the result by line 4	**5**	75
6	Charitable deduction (attach Schedule O, Form 706) and marital deduction (attach Schedule M, Form 706, and computation)	**6**	0
7	State death tax deduction (see instructions)	**7**	0
8	Total deductions. Add lines 5, 6, and 7	**8**	75
9	Taxable estate. Subtract line 8 from line 1. Enter here and on line 1 of Part II	**9**	149,925

Form **706-NA** (Rev. 8-2013)

your worldwide assets to the IRS, take the $60,000 exemption that would otherwise be available if not for the Treaty.

As described in Chapter 2, if your assets exceed the exemption amount ($5,430,000 in 2015), consider owning the assets in a Canadian entity to completely avoid US estate tax. Of course there are extra costs in doing this; this strategy is not recommended unless you would otherwise be subject to US estate tax.

> **Example 2:** Let's say that John and Jane Doe are married and their worldwide assets total $12,000,000, and they have $5,000,000 or 41.67 percent of those assets in an office building in Fort Lauderdale, Florida. The Does' credit would be $885,821 ($2,125,800 x 41.67 percent). If one of them dies and leaves the building to the spouse, they would be entitled to the Canadian Marital Credit (Line 9) that would add another $885,821 of credit. There was $15,000 in final expenses that could be reported on the US estate tax return, leaving a taxable US estate of $4,993,750 (see Schedule B of Form 706-NA). Tax on $4,993,750 is $1,943,300 before the credits. After subtracting $1,771,642 ($885,821 x 2) from the gross estate tax, you have $177,658 of US estate tax on $5,000,000 of assets, for an effective tax rate of 3.55 percent. Of course, this is with no planning at all; with some planning the US estate tax can be reduced substantially or even eliminated. See Sample 9.

3. A Dollar Is Not Always a Dollar

You would think that reporting the fair market value of real estate would be a straightforward process, but it can be very complicated. You may also be surprised to know that the way you hold title to a property can influence the fair market value. This section begins by defining terms which are different between the two countries. It ends by discussing how holding the property in an entity such as a partnership or corporation may reduce the value for estate planning purposes and therefore potentially reduce any US estate tax payable.

Sample 9
United States Estate (and Generation-Skipping Transfer) Tax Return (Form 706-NA) (Example 2)

Form **706-NA**	**United States Estate (and Generation-Skipping Transfer) Tax Return**	
(Rev. August 2013)	**Estate of nonresident not a citizen of the United States**	OMB No. 1545-0531
Department of the Treasury Internal Revenue Service	**To be filed for decedents dying after December 31, 2011.** ▶ Information about Form 706-NA and its separate instructions is at *www.irs.gov/form706na.*	

Attach supplemental documents and translations. Show amounts in U.S. dollars.

Part I Decedent, Executor, and Attorney

1a Decedent's first (given) name and middle initial	b Decedent's last (family) name	2 U.S. taxpayer ID number (if any)
John	Doe	987-65-4321

3 Place of death	4 Domicile at time of death	5 Citizenship (nationality)	6 Date of death
Canada	Canada	Canadian	02/02/2016

7a Date of birth	b Place of birth	8 Business or occupation
02/02/1930	Canada	Retired

		9a Name of executor	10a Name of attorney for estate
In United States	b Address		b Address
Outside United States	11a Name of executor		12a Name of attorney for estate
	b Address (City or town, state or province, country, and ZIP or foreign postal code.)		b Address (City or town, state or province, country, and ZIP or foreign postal code.)

Part II Tax Computation

1	Taxable estate from Schedule B, line 9	**1**	4,993,750
2	Total taxable gifts of tangible or intangible property located in the U.S., transferred (directly or indirectly) by the decedent after December 31, 1976, and not included in the gross estate (see section 2511)	**2**	0
3	Total. Add lines 1 and 2	**3**	4,993,750
4	Tentative tax on the amount on line 3 (see instructions)	**4**	1,943,300
5	Tentative tax on the amount on line 2 (see instructions)	**5**	0
6	Gross estate tax. Subtract line 5 from line 4	**6**	1,943,300
7	Unified credit. Enter smaller of line 6 amount or maximum allowed (see instructions)	**7**	885,821
8	Balance. Subtract line 7 from line 6	**8**	1,057,479
9	Other credits (see instructions) **9** 885,821		
10	Credit for tax on prior transfers. Attach Schedule Q, Form 706 . . . . . **10** 0		
11	Total. Add lines 9 and 10	**11**	885,821
12	Net estate tax. Subtract line 11 from line 8	**12**	171,658
13	Total generation-skipping transfer tax. Attach Schedule R, Form 706	**13**	0
14	**Total transfer taxes.** Add lines 12 and 13	**14**	171,658
15	Earlier payments. See instructions and attach explanation	**15**	0
16	Balance due. Subtract line 15 from line 14 (see instructions)	**16**	171,658

Under penalties of perjury, I declare that I have examined this return, including accompanying schedules and statements, and to the best of my knowledge and belief, it is true, correct, and complete. I understand that a complete return requires listing all property constituting the part of the decedent's gross estate (as defined by the statute) situated in the United States. Declaration of preparer other than the executor is based on all information of which preparer has any knowledge.

Sign Here

▶ Signature of executor _____ ▶ Date _____

▶ Signature of executor _____ ▶ Date _____

Paid Preparer Use Only	Print/Type preparer's name	Preparer's signature	Date	Check ☐ if self-employed	PTIN
	Firm's name ▶			Firm's EIN ▶	
	Firm's address ▶			Phone no.	

For Privacy Act and Paperwork Reduction Act Notice, see the separate instructions.   Cat. No. 10145K   Form **706-NA** (Rev. 8-2013)

Sample 9 — Continued

Part III General Information

		Yes	No
1a	Did the decedent die testate?		✓
b	Were letters testamentary or of administration granted for the estate?		✓
	If granted to persons other than those filing the return, include names and addresses on page 1.		
2	Did the decedent, at the time of death, own any:		
a	Real property located in the United States? .	✓	
b	U.S. corporate stock?		✓
c	Debt obligations of (1) a U.S. person, or (2) the United States, a state or any political subdivision, or the District of Columbia? .		✓
d	Other property located in the United States? .		✓
3	Was the decedent engaged in business in the United States at the date of death? . . .	✓	
4	At the date of death, did the decedent have access, personally or through an agent, to a safe deposit box located in the United States?		✓
5	At the date of death, did the decedent own any property located in the United States as a joint tenant with right of survivorship; as a tenant by the entirety; or, with surviving spouse, as community property? . . .	✓	
	If "Yes," attach Schedule E, Form 706.		
6a	Had the decedent ever been a citizen or resident of the United States (see instructions)? . . .		✓
b	If "Yes," did the decedent lose U.S. citizenship or residency within 10 years of death? (see instructions)		✓

		Yes	No
7	Did the decedent make any transfer (of property that was located in the United States at either the time of the transfer or the time of death) described in sections 2035, 2036, 2037, or 2038 (see the instructions for Form 706, Schedule G)?		✓
	If "Yes," attach Schedule G, Form 706.		
8	At the date of death, were there any trusts in existence that were created by the decedent and that included property located in the United States either when the trust was created or when the decedent died? . . .		✓
	If "Yes," attach Schedule G, Form 706.		
9	At the date of death, did the decedent:		
a	Have a general power of appointment over any property located in the United States? .		✓
b	Or, at any time, exercise or release the power?		✓
	If "Yes" to either a or b, attach Schedule H, Form 706.		
10a	Have federal gift tax returns ever been filed? .		✓
b	Periods covered ▶ ----		
c	IRS offices where filed ▶		
11	Does the gross estate in the United States include any interests in property transferred to a "skip person" as defined in the instructions to Schedule R of Form 706?		✓
	If "Yes," attach Schedules R and/or R-1, Form 706.		

Schedule A. Gross Estate in the United States (see instructions)

	Yes	No
Do you elect to value the decedent's gross estate at a date or dates after the decedent's death (as authorized by section 2032)? ▶		✓

To make the election, you must check this box "Yes." If you check "Yes," complete **all** columns. If you check "No," complete columns (a), (b), and (e); you may leave columns (c) and (d) blank or you may use them to expand your column (b) description.

(a) Item no.	(b) Description of property and securities For securities, give CUSIP number	(c) Alternate valuation date	(d) Alternate value in U.S. dollars	(e) Value at date of death in U.S. dollars
1	Office Building in Fort Lauderdale, Florida	N/A	N/A	5,000,000
	(If you need more space, attach additional sheets of same size.)			
Total	. . . .		N/A	5,000,000

Schedule B. Taxable Estate

Caution. You must document lines 2 and 4 for the deduction on line 5 to be allowed.

1	Gross estate in the United States (Schedule A total)	1	5,000,000
2	Gross estate outside the United States (see instructions)	2	7,000,000
3	Entire gross estate wherever located. Add amounts on lines 1 and 2	3	12,000,000
4	Amount of funeral expenses, administration expenses, decedent's debts, mortgages and liens, and losses during administration. Attach itemized schedule. (see instructions)	4	15,000
5	Deduction for expenses, claims, etc. Divide line 1 by line 3 and multiply the result by line 4 . . .	5	6,250
6	Charitable deduction (attach Schedule O, Form 706) and marital deduction (attach Schedule M, Form 706, and computation)	6	0
7	State death tax deduction (see instructions)	7	0
8	Total deductions. Add lines 5, 6, and 7	8	6,250
9	Taxable estate. Subtract line 8 from line 1. Enter here and on line 1 of Part II	9	4,993,750

Form **706-NA** (Rev. 8-2013)

When reporting the value of your US assets, you must use the fair market value (FMV). The definitions of FMV are different in the US and Canada.

Table 8
Unified Estate and Gift Tax Rate Schedule

Column A Taxable amount over	Column B Taxable amount not over	Column C Tax on amount in Column A	Column D Rate of tax on excess over amount in Column A
$0	$10,000	$0	18 percent
$10,000	$20,000	$1,800	20 percent
$20,000	$40,000	$3,800	22 percent
$40,000	$60,000	$8,200	24 percent
$60,000	$80,000	$13,000	26 percent
$80,000	$100,000	$18,200	28 percent
$100,000	$150,000	$23,800	30 percent
$150,000	$250,000	$38,800	32 percent
$250,000	$500,000	$70,800	34 percent
$500,000	$750,000	$155,800	37 percent
$750,000	$1,000,000	$248,300	39 percent
$1,000,000	-------------	$345,800	40 percent

In United States tax law, the definition of *fair market value* is found in the United States Supreme Court decision in the *Cartwright* case:

The fair market value is the price at which the property would change hands between a willing buyer and a willing seller, neither being under any compulsion to buy or to sell and both having reasonable knowledge of relevant facts.

The term *fair market value* is used throughout the Internal Revenue Code and among other federal statutory laws in the US including bankruptcy, many state laws, and several regulatory bodies.

In Canada, the term *fair market value* is not explicitly defined in the *Income Tax Act*. That said, Mr. Justice Cattanach in *Henderson Estate, Bank of New York v. M.N.R.*, (1973) C.T.C. 636 at p. 644 articulates the concept as follows:

The statute does not define the expression "fair market value," but the expression has been defined in many different ways depending generally on the subject matter which the person seeking to define it had in mind. I do not think it necessary to attempt an exact definition of the expression as used in the statute other than to say that the words must be construed in accordance with the common understanding of them. That common understanding I take to mean the highest price an asset might reasonably be expected to bring if sold by the owner in the normal method applicable to the asset in question in the ordinary course of business in a market not exposed to any undue stresses and composed of willing buyers and sellers dealing at arm's length and under no compulsion to buy or sell. I would add that the foregoing understanding as I have expressed it in a general way includes what I conceive to be the essential element which is an open and unrestricted market in which the price is hammered out between willing and informed buyers and sellers on the anvil of supply and demand. These definitions are equally applicable to "fair market value" and "market value" and it is doubtful if the word "fair" adds anything to the words "market value."

Canada Revenue Agency (CRA) lists the following definition in its online dictionary:

Fair market value generally means the highest price, expressed in dollars, that a property would bring in an open and unrestricted market between a willing buyer and a willing seller who are both knowledgeable, informed, and prudent, and who are acting independently of each other.

As you can see, the US and Canadian concepts of fair market value are very similar, but not exactly the same.

That being said, there are a number of factors that influence what a buyer is willing to pay. A couple of the more common factors are a lack of control and a lack of marketability (liquidity). If one or both of these factors exist, a discount is applied before arriving at FMV.

The discount for lack of control is pretty straightforward. Would you pay the same amount for an asset over which you had no or very little say as you would for an asset which you can control? Here is an example: Most people would readily exchange one dollar for another dollar (i.e., provide me change for my loonie) if there were no restriction on what they could do with that dollar. It would elicit an entirely different response if I asked for change for my loonie, but told you that you could not spend that dollar without my permission.

The liquidity discount or liquid asset has some or more of the following features according to Wikipedia (July, 2015):

It can be sold rapidly, with minimal loss of value, any time within market hours. The essential characteristic of a liquid market is that there are ready and willing buyers and sellers at all times. Another elegant definition of liquidity is the probability that the next trade is executed at a price equal to the last one. A market may be considered deeply liquid if there are ready and willing buyers and sellers in large quantities. This is related to the concept of market depth that can be measured as the units that can be sold or bought for a given price impact. The opposite concept is that of market breadth measured as the price impact per unit of liquidity.

An illiquid asset is an asset which is not readily salable due to uncertainty about its value or the lack of a market in which it is regularly traded. The mortgage related assets which resulted in the subprime mortgage crisis are examples of illiquid assets, as their value is not readily determinable despite being secured by real property. Another example is an asset such as a large block of stock, the sale of which affects the market value.

When holding your real estate in a business entity in which the other business owners cannot readily sell their shares or membership interests and do not own a greater than 50 percent interest in the business, you will most likely receive a discount for both of these factors (lack of marketability and minority discounts). The discounts applied vary based on the facts and circumstances of the business, but a common combined discount is 30 percent. Therefore, if you have real estate valued in the partnership at $100,000 and assuming no other assets in the partnership, the value of the partnership might be around $70,000 if these discounts are applied. The $70,000 is the number you would report as the value of your US assets on an estate tax return. An appraisal from a qualified appraiser is required to prove the discount.

Tip: Holding assets in a business entity may reduce your US estate tax liability due to valuation discounts.

4. Probate

Probate is the legal process of administering the estate of a deceased person by resolving all claims and distributing the deceased person's property under a valid will.

Probate generally lasts several months, and it can take over a year before all of the property is distributed. Costs can range from minimal to expensive, depending on the state and the complexity of the probate. One complexity that may come up with some regularity is having a Quebec will. Not only might the will be in French and therefore require official translation, it is based on Napoleonic law versus common law used elsewhere.

Avoiding probate can be accomplished by having the property pass directly to heirs contractually, such as through a beneficiary designation like those of insurance policies or retirement plans. Property can also pass contractually when it is owned jointly with rights of survivorship. There are things that can be done with bank and brokerage accounts that are very much like naming a beneficiary and it is called owning the property as "payable on death." Just like a beneficiary designation, you can name and/ or change beneficiaries at any time prior to death. If married, changes can be made prior to the survivor's death. This concept is very similar to beneficiary deeds described in Chapter 2.

Note: If you have a bank account in the US that is not held in an entity such as a corporation or partnership, you should consider setting up Paid on Death (POD) accounts to avoid probate.

Another way to avoid probate is to establish a revocable living trust. Any assets held in the trust pass to beneficiaries by the terms of the trust. Another advantage of revocable living trusts is that they are private. Since the trust is not filed with the court and there is no need for probate, all the terms of the trust are kept private. However, a will is a public document that can be viewed by anyone after the person has died and the probate has been settled.

As I mentioned in Chapter 2, a revocable living trust may not be necessary if the property is in a state that allows beneficiary deeds. It would also not be needed if the property is held in some sort of foreign entity such as a corporation or partnership. Lastly, the revocable living trust would not be needed for small properties in which the cost of probate would be less than the cost of the trust.

Caution: Be very careful about adding children to the title as joint owners to avoid probate. While this strategy will certainly avoid probate, it creates a whole host of other, potentially worse problems. The first such problem would be potential gift tax consequences. If you add a child as a joint owner, you may have just gifted half the value of the property to the child. In addition, you subject the property to the claims of the children, such as divorce, bankruptcy, lawsuits, etc.

4.1 State-specific rules of probate

Arizona and Florida do not regulate probate fees, but they must be "reasonable." Arizona requires a four-month period in which to present a claim against the estate, therefore no Arizona probate can be completed in less than four months. In Florida, the minimum time is three months.

California sets the maximum fees that attorneys can charge for probate. The fees are:

- 4 percent of the first $100,000 of the estate,

- 3 percent of the next $100,000,

- 2 percent of the next $800,000,

- 1 percent of the next $9,000,000, and

- 0.5 percent of the next $15,000,000.

The court will determine the fee for amounts greater than $25,000,000.

If the executor receives a fee, he or she will be paid according to the same fee schedule, effectively doubling the fees. If there are complications, the attorney and executor can ask the judge to approve higher fees. There are also various court fees that typically run about $1,000 to $3,000. Probate in California will take, at a minimum, about nine months to be completed.

5

Other Things You Need to Know

When buying real estate anywhere, there are more things to consider than simply the purchase price and how to take title. Other issues expand when buying property in a foreign country. A few of the issues you should consider before investing in the US are:

- Are there any filing requirements that are not related to federal or state income tax?

- Should I be charging a sales tax on any rent I will be charging?

- What potential liability do I have and how do the civil laws in the US work?

- Am I liable for only my US assets or can the creditor go after my Canadian assets, and if so, under what circumstances?

- If borrowing, should the loan be in US or Canadian dollars?

- How should I handle the conversion of currency?

- How can I tell a good property manager from a bad one?

- How do I screen property managers?

1. Other Filing Requirements

1.1. Department of Commerce filing requirements

A series of forms that are frequently overlooked are those from the Bureau of Economic Analysis (BEA), a division of the US Department of Commerce. These forms are typically not completed by advisors because of their obscurity and by the fact that they are not tax forms; accountants generally do not consider it their responsibility.

The BEA produces statistics on foreign direct investment in the US. The statistics, which are the world's most comprehensive and accurate, are obtained from mandatory surveys. Even if you are exempt from annual filing, you are still required to file Claim for Exemption (Form BE-15), to prove your exemption. In other words, even if you would have been exempt except for the fact you failed to file the Claim for Exemption, you are liable for all of the penalties and possible imprisonment; same as a company that is not exempt. (See Sample 10.)

To be eligible for exemption, your "total assets, sales or operating revenues, or net income, have to be $40 million or less, for the fiscal year that ended in calendar year 2015." This makes virtually everyone reading this book exempt, if they file Form BE-15. See Table 9 for the proper BE-15 form to file.

Note that if you are buying the property for personal use (i.e., not for a business reason), you are exempt and do not have to file the claim for exemption.

1.1a Filing requirements

Filers must:

- be a foreign person (see below),

- have direct or indirect ownership interest of at least 10 percent of the voting stock, or equivalent,

Claim for Exemption (Form BE-15)

FORM **BE-15 Claim for Exemption** (REV1/2014)

OMB No. 0608-0034: Approval Expires 11/30/2018

BE-15 Identification Number

◼BEA
BUREAU OF ECONOMIC ANALYSIS
U.S. DEPARTMENT OF COMMERCE

2014 ANNUAL SURVEY OF FOREIGN DIRECT INVESTMENT
IN THE UNITED STATES
CLAIM FOR EXEMPTION FROM FILING FORM BE-15A, BE-15B, OR BE-15C

Due date: May 31, 2015

Electronic filing:
www.bea.gov/efile

Mail reports to:
U.S. Department of Commerce
Bureau of Economic Analysis
Direct Investment Division, BE–49(A)
4600 Silver Hill Rd
Washington, DC 20233

Deliver reports to:
U.S. Department of Commerce
Bureau of Economic Analysis
Direct Investment Division, BE–49(A)
4600 Silver Hill Rd
Suitland, MD 20746

Fax reports to:
(301) 278–9500

Response Required

Name and address of U.S. business enterprise

1002 Name of U.S. affiliate
0

1010 c/o (care of)
0

1003 Street or P.O. Box
0

1004 City
0   0998 State

1005 ZIP Code
0   OR   Foreign Postal Code

Assistance: E-mail: be12/15@bea.gov
Telephone: (301) 278-9247
Copies of blank forms: www.bea.gov/fdi

Include your BE-15 Identification Number with all requests.

All persons who are contacted by BEA about reporting in this survey, either by sending them forms or by written inquiry, must respond pursuant to Section 801.3 of 15 CFR pt. 801 and the survey instructions. They may respond by:
- filing the properly completed Form BE-15A, BE-15B, or BE-15C by May 31, 2015;
- completing and returning the Form BE-15 Claim for Exemption from Filing Form BE-15A, BE-15B, or BE-15C, by May 31, 2015;
- certifying in writing, by May 31, 2015, to the fact that the person had no direct investment within the purview of the reporting requirements of the BE-15 survey.

Mandatory Confidentiality Penalties
This survey is being conducted under the International Investment and Trade in Services Survey Act (P.L. 94–472, 90 Stat. 2059, 22 U.S.C. 3101–3108, as amended). The filing of reports is mandatory and the Act provides that your report to this Bureau is confidential. Whoever fails to report may be subject to penalties. See page 4 for more details.

CONTACT INFORMATION
Provide information of person to consult about this report:

Name
0
1000

Street 1
0
1029

Telephone Number
0
1001

Extension

Street 2
0
1030

Fax Number
0
0990

City   State   Zip
0
1001

E-mail Address
0
1028

NOTE: BEA uses a Secure Messaging System to correspond with you via encrypted message to discuss questions relating to this form. We may use your e-mail address for survey-related announcements and to inform you about secure messages. When communicating with BEA by e-mail, please do not include any confidential business or personal information.

CERTIFICATION

The undersigned official certifies that this report has been prepared in accordance with the applicable instructions, is complete, and is substantially accurate including estimates that may have been provided.

Signature of Authorized Official   Date   Telephone Number
0   0992   0

Extension
0

Name
0
0990

Title
0
0991

Fax Number
0
0993

Sample 10 — Continued

WHICH SECTIONS TO COMPLETE?

Provide the name and address of U.S. business enterprise, the person to consult concerning questions about this report, and the certification on page 1. Also, review the questions below to determine the additional information required.

I Were at least 10 percent of the voting rights in your business enterprise directly or indirectly owned by a foreign person or entity at the end of your fiscal year that ended in calendar year 2014?

☐ Yes – Continue with question II.

☐ No – Complete item 2(a) or (b) or (c) or (e) on page 3. If your business has been liquidated or dissolved, complete (a) or (b). Do not complete questions II, III or IV.

II Were more than 50 percent of the voting rights in this U.S. business enterprise owned by another U.S. affiliate, or was this U.S. business enterprise merged into another U.S. affiliate before the end of this U.S. business enterprise's fiscal year that ended in calendar year 2014? Note: U.S. affiliate is defined on page 4.

☐ Yes – Continue with question III.

☐ No – Skip to question IV.

III Will the data for this U.S. business enterprise be consolidated into the 2014 BE-15 report filed for the U.S. affiliate that owns it more than 50 percent, or be included on the 2014 BE-15 report filed for the U.S. affiliate into which it was merged?

☐ Yes – Complete item 2d(1) or 2d(2) on page 3.

☐ No – Contact BEA for guidance.

IV Did **any one** of the items – Total assets, Sales or gross operating revenues, or Net income (loss) – for the U.S. affiliate (not just the foreign parent's share) exceed **$40 million** at the end of, or for, its fiscal year that ended in calendar year 2014?

☐ Yes – You are not eligible to file Form BE-15 Claim for Exemption and must file either a Form BE-15A, BE-15B, or BE-15C. Copies of blank forms can be found at: **www.bea.gov/fdi**

☐ No – Complete items 1a through 1h. Do NOT complete page 3.

BASIS OF CLAIM FOR EXEMPTION

Select ONE type of exemption -- either based on Value (#1 below) or based on one of the reasons listed under Other Exemptions (#2 on page 3). Please check box corresponding to the type of exemption you are claiming.

(1) ☐ **Exemption based on Value. Complete if item IV was "NO".**

Rounding – Report currency amounts in U.S. dollars rounded to thousands (omitting 000). **Do not enter amounts in the shaded portions of each line.**
Example – If amount is $1,334,891.00 report as: ....

	$ Bil.	Mil.	Thous.	Dols.
		1	335	000

	$ Bil.	Mil.	Thous.	Dols.
(a) Total assets at the close of the fiscal year that ended in calendar year 2014 – Do not net out liabilities.......... 2109				000
(b) Sales or gross operating revenues for the fiscal year that ended in calendar year 2014, excluding sales taxes – Do not give gross margin.......... 2149				000
(c) Net income (loss) for the fiscal year that ended in calendar year 2014, after provision for U.S. Federal, state, and local income taxes. 2159				000
(d) Total liabilities at the close of the fiscal year that ended in calendar year 2014.......... 2114				000

☐ **Please check box if total liabilities are zero.**

(e) Major product(s) or service(s) of the fully consolidated domestic U.S. affiliate – Briefly describe the major product(s) and/or service(s) of the U.S. affiliate. If a product, also state what is done to it, i.e., whether it is mined, manufactured, sold at wholesale, transported, packaged, etc. (For example, "manufacture widgets.")

1163

(f) Industry code of the fully consolidated domestic U.S. affiliate – Enter the 4-digit International Surveys Industry(ISI) code of the industry with the largest sales or gross operating revenues. For a full explanation of each code, see the *Guide to Industry Classifications for International Surveys, 2012.* A copy of this guide can be found on our web site at: www.bea.gov/naics2012

ISI Code
--Select ISI CODE-- 1164

(g) Enter the country in which the foreign parent is incorporated or organized, if a business enterprise, or is resident, if an individual or government. The foreign parent is the FIRST person or entity outside the U.S. in a chain of ownership that has a 10 percent or more **voting** interest in this U.S. affiliate. See diagram on page 4 for an illustration of foreign parent.

BEA USE ONLY

Country of foreign parent
--Select Country-- 3016

(h) Enter the country in which the ultimate beneficial owner (UBO) is incorporated or organized, if a business enterprise, or is resident, if an individual or government. The UBO is that person or entity, proceeding up the ownership chain beginning with and including the foreign parent, that is not more than 50 percent owned or controlled by another person or entity. See diagram on page 4 for an illustration of UBO.

BEA USE ONLY

Country of UBO
--Select Country-- 3022

FORM BE-15 Claim For Exemption (REV 1/2014)   Page 2

Check ONE box corresponding to the type of exemption you are claiming.

This U.S. business enterprise is exempt from filing a Form BE-15A, BE-15B, or BE-15C because:

(2) Other exemptions (check box below)

(a) 0170 1 ☐ This U.S. business enterprise was a U.S. affiliate of a foreign person or entity at some time during calendar year 2014, but ceased to be a U.S. affiliate before the end of the fiscal year that ended in calendar year 2014.

Give date foreign ownership ceased or went below 10 percent, or when the business was liquidated or dissolved.

7012 | mm/dd/yyyy

(b) 0110 1 ☐ This U.S. business enterprise was not a U.S. affiliate of a foreign person or entity at any time during calendar year 2014, but had been a U.S. affiliate of a foreign person at some time before January 1, 2014.

Give date foreign ownership ceased or went below 10 percent, or when the business was liquidated or dissolved.

7010 | mm/dd/yyyy

(c) 0180 1 ☐ This U.S. business enterprise is a U.S. affiliate of a foreign person or entity, but became a U.S. affiliate after the end of its fiscal year that ended in calendar year 2014, or if a newly formed company, its first fiscal year did not or will not end until after the end of calendar year 2014.

Complete items (1) and (2).

(1) *Give date when the U.S. business enterprise became a U.S. affiliate of a foreign person.*

7013 | mm/dd/yyyy

(2) *Give the ending date of the U.S. business enterprise's fiscal year that ended in calendar year 2014. If a newly formed company, give the ending date of the U.S. business enterprise's first fiscal year. NOTE: For a newly formed company this must be a date in calendar year 2015.*

7014 | mm/dd/yyyy

(d) This U.S. business enterprise was controlled by a U.S. affiliate of a foreign person or entity during the fiscal year that ended in calendar year 2014 and is (check appropriate box (1) or (2)):

(1) 0112 1 ☐ **Fully consolidated** into the 2014 BE-15 report filed for that U.S. affiliate;

OR

(2) 0112 2 ☐ **Merged** into, and included on the 2014 BE-15 report filed for, that U.S. affiliate.

On the lines below give the name, address, and BE-15 Identification Number of the U.S. affiliate into which this U.S. business enterprise is fully consolidated or merged.

0120 Name 0

0130 Street or 0

0140 City 0 | 0141 State 0 | 0150 Zip Code 0

7011 BE-15 Identification Number 0

(e) 0190 1 1 ☐ Other – Specify and include reference to section of regulations or instructions on which claim is based – attach remarks on a separate sheet if necessary.

7015 0

Sample 10 — Continued

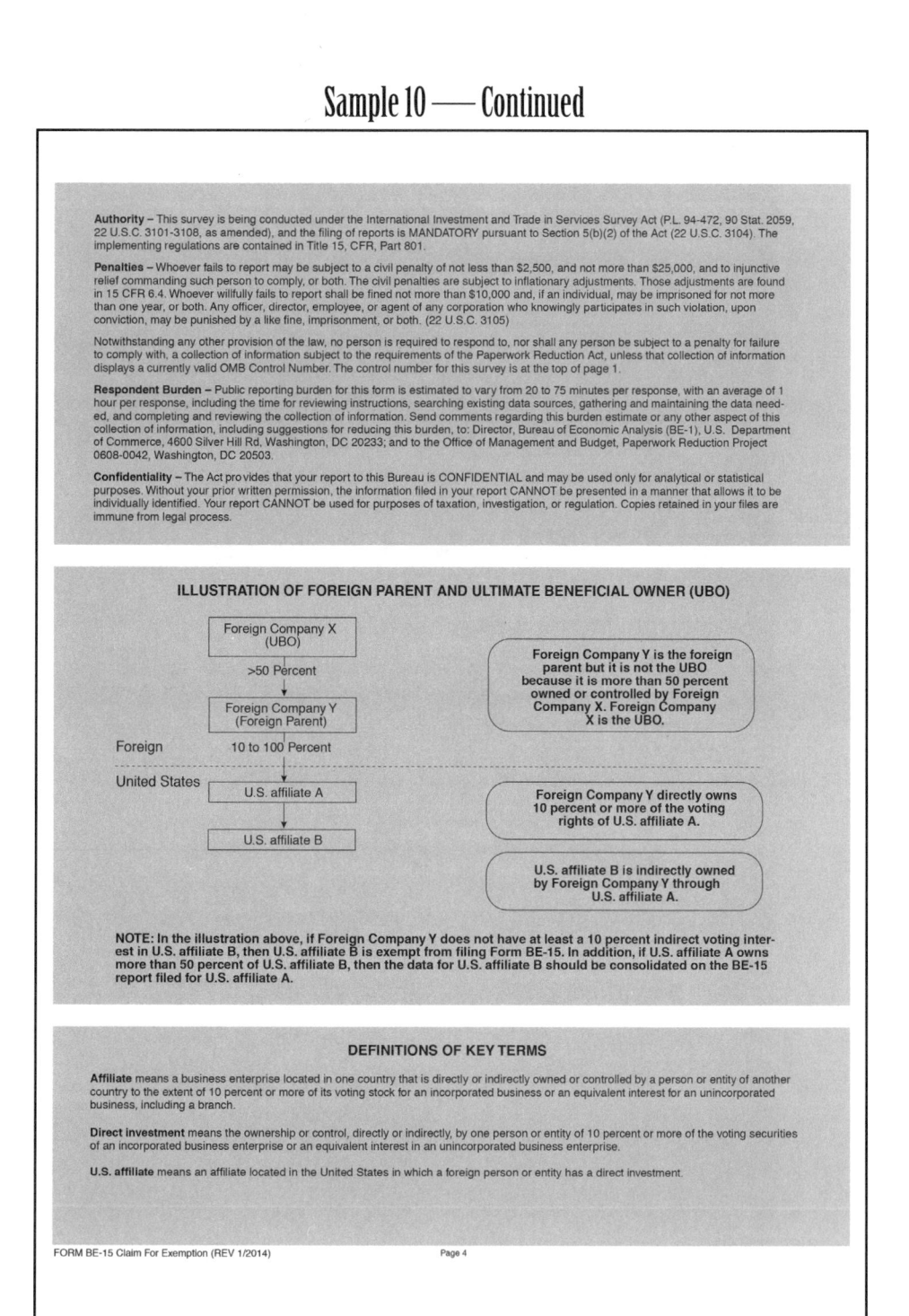

Authority – This survey is being conducted under the International Investment and Trade in Services Survey Act (P.L. 94-472, 90 Stat. 2059, 22 U.S.C. 3101-3108, as amended), and the filing of reports is MANDATORY pursuant to Section 5(b)(2) of the Act (22 U.S.C. 3104). The implementing regulations are contained in Title 15, CFR, Part 801.

Penalties – Whoever fails to report may be subject to a civil penalty of not less than $2,500, and not more than $25,000, and to injunctive relief commanding such person to comply, or both. The civil penalties are subject to inflationary adjustments. Those adjustments are found in 15 CFR 6.4. Whoever willfully fails to report shall be fined not more than $10,000, and, if an individual, may be imprisoned for not more than one year, or both. Any officer, director, employee, or agent of any corporation who knowingly participates in such violation, upon conviction, may be punished by a like fine, imprisonment, or both. (22 U.S.C. 3105)

Notwithstanding any other provision of the law, no person is required to respond to, nor shall any person be subject to a penalty for failure to comply with, a collection of information subject to the requirements of the Paperwork Reduction Act, unless that collection of information displays a currently valid OMB Control Number. The control number for this survey is at the top of page 1.

Respondent Burden – Public reporting burden for this form is estimated to vary from 20 to 75 minutes per response, with an average of 1 hour per response, including the time for reviewing instructions, searching existing data sources, gathering and maintaining the data need-ed, and completing and reviewing the collection of information. Send comments regarding this burden estimate or any other aspect of this collection of information, including suggestions for reducing this burden, to: Director, Bureau of Economic Analysis (BE-1), U.S. Department of Commerce, 4600 Silver Hill Rd, Washington, DC 20233; and to the Office of Management and Budget, Paperwork Reduction Project 0608-0042, Washington, DC 20503.

Confidentiality – The Act provides that your report to this Bureau is CONFIDENTIAL and may be used only for analytical or statistical purposes. Without your prior written permission, the information filed in your report CANNOT be presented in a manner that allows it to be individually identified. Your report CANNOT be used for purposes of taxation, investigation, or regulation. Copies retained in your files are immune from legal process.

ILLUSTRATION OF FOREIGN PARENT AND ULTIMATE BENEFICIAL OWNER (UBO)

Foreign Company X (UBO)

>50 Percent

Foreign Company Y (Foreign Parent)

Foreign

10 to 100 Percent

United States

U.S. affiliate A

U.S. affiliate B

Foreign Company Y is the foreign parent but it is not the UBO because it is more than 50 percent owned or controlled by Foreign Company X. Foreign Company X is the UBO.

Foreign Company Y directly owns 10 percent or more of the voting rights of U.S. affiliate A.

U.S. affiliate B is indirectly owned by Foreign Company Y through U.S. affiliate A.

NOTE: In the illustration above, if Foreign Company Y does not have at least a 10 percent indirect voting inter-est in U.S. affiliate B, then U.S. affiliate B is exempt from filing Form BE-15. In addition, if U.S. affiliate A owns more than 50 percent of U.S. affiliate B, then the data for U.S. affiliate B should be consolidated on the BE-15 report filed for U.S. affiliate A.

DEFINITIONS OF KEY TERMS

Affiliate means a business enterprise located in one country that is directly or indirectly owned or controlled by a person or entity of another country to the extent of 10 percent or more of its voting stock for an incorporated business or an equivalent interest for an unincorporated business, including a branch.

Direct investment means the ownership or control, directly or indirectly, by one person or entity of 10 percent or more of the voting securities of an incorporated business enterprise or an equivalent interest in an unincorporated business enterprise.

U.S. affiliate means an affiliate located in the United States in which a foreign person or entity has a direct investment.

FORM BE-15 Claim For Exemption (REV 1/2014)   Page 4

- file electronically at www.bea.gov/efile, and

- file by May 31 or June 30 if e-filing.

For inquiries, call 202-606-5615 or email at be12_15@bea.gov.

Caution: A "foreign person" is defined as anyone who is a resident outside the US and subject to the jurisdiction of another country. That means that if you are a US citizen or green card holder living in Canada and investing in US real estate for business purposes, you are required to complete these forms.

The following information is from one of the forms (BE-15) that are required to be completed. *"Whoever fails to report is subject to a civil penalty of not less than $2,500 and not more than $25,000 … The civil penalties are subject to inflationary adjustments. Whoever fails to report shall be fined not more than $10,000 … may be imprisoned for not more than one year, or both.*

The law provides that your survey is confidential and may be used only for analytical or statistical purposes. The information cannot be presented in a manner that allows it to be individually identified. Your report cannot be used for purposes of taxation, investigation, or regulation. Copies retained by the Bureau are immune from the legal process."

Obviously, with a $40 million threshold, a very large portion of the investors in US real estate will qualify for the exemption. However, if the real estate is being used for business (rented) you must file Form BE-15. Consider going to a different advisor if your advisor is either not aware of the BEA forms or is unwilling to prepare them for you.

2. Other Filings

If you are renting out your property, the rent may be subject to sales tax. When sales tax would have to be imposed and how much depends on where the property is located and how many properties you have. In Arizona, for example, most cities do not impose a sales tax if only one single family home is rented; sometimes you can have as many as three properties before sales tax is required. Note that if you are renting a commercial building or an apartment complex, you will always be required to pay sales tax.

Arizona Department of Revenue requires that owners of residential rental property file a form (Registration of Arizona Residential Rental Property) with the assessor of the county in which the property is located. Penalty for failure to file can be up to $1,000, plus $100 per month.

In California and Florida, the registration requirement seems to be at the city level, when required. Ask your realtor or tax advisor for details.

2.1 California Proposition 13

Under Proposition 13 tax reform, property tax value was rolled back and frozen at the 1976 assessed value level. Property tax increases on any given property were limited to no more than 2 percent, per year, as long as the property was not sold. Once sold, the property was reassessed at 1 percent of the sale price, and the 2 percent yearly cap became applicable to future years. This allowed property owners to finally be able to estimate the amount of future property taxes, and determine the maximum amount taxes could increase as long as he or she owned the property.

What you need to know:

1. One percent rate cap: Proposition 13 capped, with limited exceptions, *ad valorem* property tax rates at one percent of full cash value at the time of acquisition. Prior to Proposition 13, local jurisdictions independently established their tax rates and the total property tax rate was the composite of the individual rates, with few limitations.

2. Annual increases limited: Annual assessments are limited to a 2 percent increase, but at no time can the total assessment exceed 1 percent of the value of the property.

3. Reassessment upon change of ownership: Proposition 13 replaced the practice of annually reassessing property at

Table 9
Which 2015 BE-15 Form to File

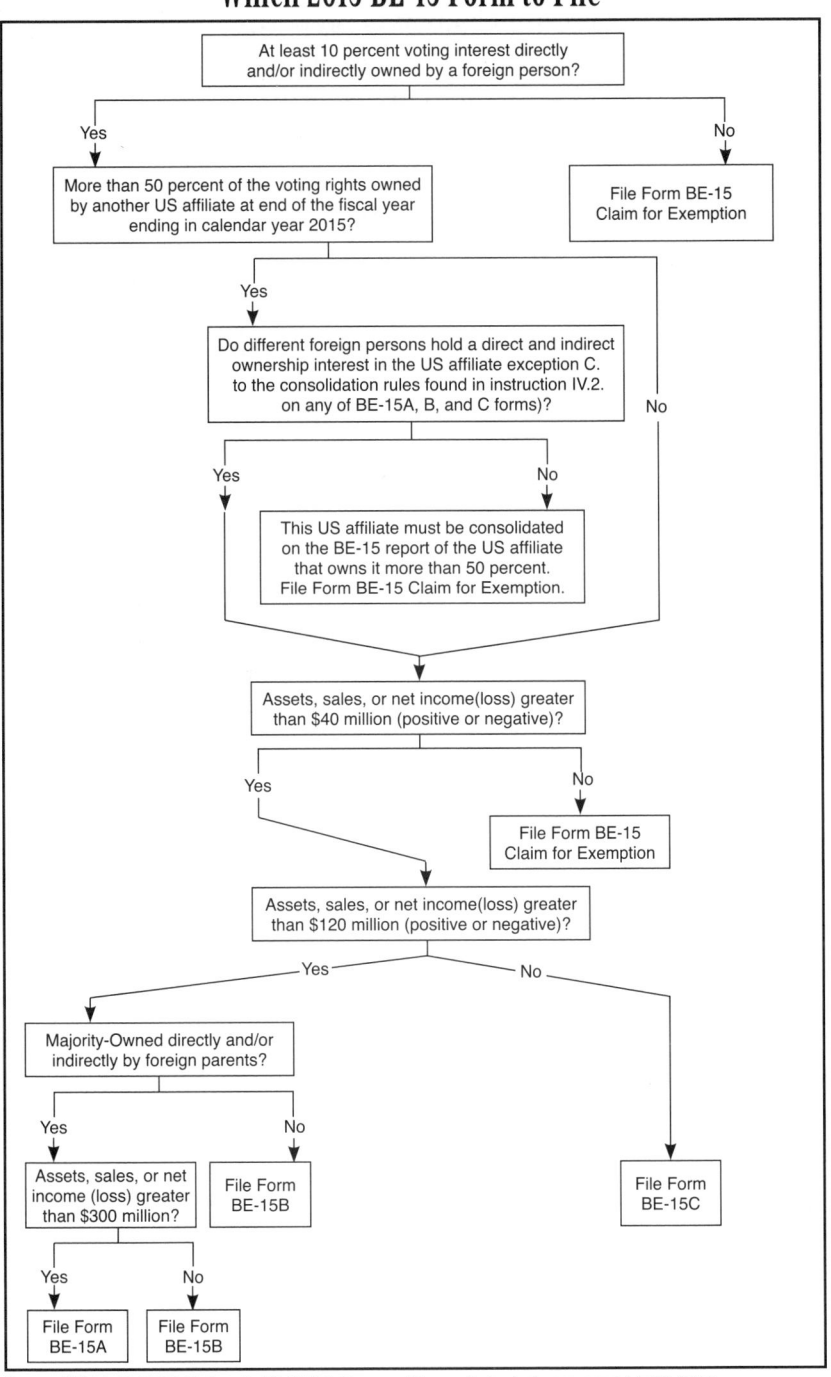

At least 10 percent voting interest directly and/or indirectly owned by a foreign person?

Yes → More than 50 percent of the voting rights owned by another US affiliate at end of the fiscal year ending in calendar year 2015?

No → File Form BE-15 Claim for Exemption

Yes → Do different foreign persons hold a direct and indirect ownership interest in the US affiliate exception C. to the consolidation rules found in instruction IV.2. on any of BE-15A, B, and C forms)?

No → This US affiliate must be consolidated on the BE-15 report of the US affiliate that owns it more than 50 percent. File Form BE-15 Claim for Exemption.

Assets, sales, or net income(loss) greater than $40 million (positive or negative)?

No → File Form BE-15 Claim for Exemption

Yes → Assets, sales, or net income(loss) greater than $120 million (positive or negative)?

Yes → Majority-Owned directly and/or indirectly by foreign parents?

No → File Form BE-15C

Yes → Assets, sales, or net income (loss) greater than $300 million?

No → File Form BE-15B

Yes → File Form BE-15A

No → File Form BE-15B

Source: "Which 2015 BE-15 Form to File?" U.S. Bureau of Economic Analysis, accessed July 22, 2016, www.bea.gov/surveys/pdf/be15/2015-annual-survey/which-form-do-i-file.pdf

market value with a system based on cost at acquisition. Prior to Proposition 13, if homes in a neighborhood sold for higher prices, neighboring properties might have been reassessed based on the newly increased area values. Under Proposition 13, the property is assessed for tax purposes only when it changes ownership. As long as the property is not sold, future increases in assessed value are limited to an annual inflation factor of no more than 2 percent.

4. Exceptions apply to reassessment upon change of ownership: The primary exceptions are the Parent-Child-Grandchild exception and transfers between spouses.

When you are buying or transferring property in California to a family member or related entity, you need to beware that the property tax assessment may increase substantially, and how to plan around such increases.

3. Overview of Issues That May Come Up in the Buying Process

The next sections cover issues that you will want to at least consider as you go through the real estate buying process.

3.1 Title insurance

While buying real estate in the US is a somewhat different process, it is basically similar to Canada and easy to do. The ease with which property can be bought in the US can be both a good and bad thing. This ease can lead investors to believe that there are no problems. The problem is that there are no warning signals when you do something the wrong way; it is just as easy to buy the property the wrong way as it is to buy it the right way. In other words, there is nothing prohibiting you from doing things the wrong way and in some cases the easiest way can be the wrong way. Revisit Chapter 2 for a discussion of the various ways to purchase property in the US, as well as the pros and cons of each.

Other than how you own the property, the biggest difference between buying real estate in the US and Canada is title insurance. Wikipedia defines title insurance as "indemnity insurance against financial loss from defects in title to real property and from the invalidity or unenforceability of mortgage liens." The insurance policy will protect an owner's interest in the real estate against loss due to title defects or liens. The insurance will defend against a lawsuit attacking the title, or reimburse the insured for the actual monetary loss incurred, up to the dollar amount of insurance provided by the policy, which is typically the purchase price of the property. First American and Fidelity National are the two largest US title companies; combined they accounted for more than 55 percent of the market in 2011. Although the cost of title insurance varies from state to state and the calculations involve numerous variables, the rule of thumb is that the cost will be approximately 0.5 percent of the purchase price of the property and is one-time cost. The cost of insurance is typically paid by the seller, but is subject to negotiation.

While title insurance is available in many other countries, such as Canada, title insurance does not constitute a significant share of the real estate transactions. While title insurance originated in the US approximately 150 years ago (in 1853 the first policy was issued and the first title company was formed in 1876), it has only become popular in Canada during the last 20 years or so.

Caution: Using a quitclaim deed to transfer property can negate the title insurance. A quitclaim deed transfers title with no guarantee that the title is good. A general warranty deed states that the title is free from any "cloud" on the ownership. A special warranty deed only claims that nothing has been done to cloud the title, but does not vouch for previous owners. I suggest that you use a special warranty deed when transferring real estate.

3.2 Finding a real estate agent

One of the biggest mistakes real estate investors make is not using a "buyer's agent" experienced in working with real estate investors. A buyer's agent is different from other real estate agents or brokers in that they do not represent sellers; some never list properties for sale and only work with buyers.

When a buyer calls the listing agent asking to see the property and eventually has that agent draw up an offer on that property, the buyer is in effect asking that agent to represent both the buyer and seller at the same time. This obviously sets up a conflict of interest called "dual agency." Some states ban dual agency, and all states require disclosures of the conflict.

To be clear, an agent has a fiduciary duty to act in the client's best interest at all times. Many would say it is impossible to work in the seller's best interest of wanting to get the best (highest) price, while at the same time, work in the buyer's best interest of wanting to get the best (lowest) price. You can find a buyer's agent at the National Buyer's Agent Association at http://buyersagent.net.

3.3 Closing costs

Closing costs in the US are quite a bit higher than those in Canada due to a number of fees, taxes, and insurance that are typically rolled in. Some of the closing fees are absorbed by the Canadian lender, but much of the difference is due to the fact the US has different closing requirements. Possible costs include pro-rata property taxes, insurance, appraisals, and inspection fees. In total, the average closing cost for a mortgage origination in Canada is roughly $1,000 USD, versus $3,700 USD in the US (Source: AllBusiness, July 2015). Bankrate.com provides a United States closing costs map that may be of interest to you; simply click on a state and it will show you the average type and amount of fees for a loan of $200,000.

3.4 US mortgages

There are US lenders that will provide a mortgage to Canadians buying property in the US. Granted there are not a large number of mortgage providers for Canadians, but there are enough to give you the ability to shop for rates and terms.

Something you should know about obtaining a US mortgage is that different rules apply to a person looking to buy a second (vacation) home versus a person looking at a property for investment. The rates and terms will be better for a second home than for an investment property. In addition, some lenders will not lend on investment property, but those that do will require a minimum down payment of 30 to 50 percent. Some lenders may require a liquid reserve of 3 to 12 months, determined on a case-by-case basis.

Some lenders you might consider talking to are:

- RBC Bank: 1-800-769-2553

- Natbank (National Bank Financial Group of Canada): 954-922-9992

- Desjardins: 1-800-454-5058

- BMO Harris Bank: 888-340-2265

- HSBC: 1-800-333-7023

- Express Capital Mortgage (mortgage broker): 800-568-0278

3.5 Foreign currency

Talking about mortgages leads naturally into foreign currency because you may run into an issue of having a mortgage (debt) in Canadian dollars, but have mortgage payments (revenue and an asset) in US dollars. When you have a situation of having to pay the Canadian mortgage every month with money coming from in from US dollars, you are at the whim of the currency markets. As I see it, there are three things you can do to reduce or eliminate that risk: pay with cash, use other Canadian money to pay the Canadian mortgage, or use a US mortgage. Of course, if the rent does not cover all of the rental expenses (have positive cash flow), you have the same problem in reverse because you are continually sending money down to the States to cover expenses.

A related issue is the expense of converting currency, which especially acute when continually transferring small amounts of money. There are really two ways in which to transfer money across the border, and they are to send checks or wire transfers. Sending checks can be problematic, in that there may be additional bank fees for accepting checks drawn on a foreign bank and there may be a hold placed on the check. In my opinion, wire transfers are the best way to go; there are few to no hassles and they are faster. When making wire transfers, there are basically two ways to go about it; you let your bank or brokerage be your currency broker, or you can use a firm that specializes in currency exchange. It has been my experience that currency brokers are the best choice because they are typically less expensive and easier to deal with.

One of the biggest problems with currency exchange is that you do not know how much the middleman is taking; these fees can be as high as 2 percent. I prefer using a company that will disclose what percentage they will charge such as MTFX. You can find live rates and the MTFX spreads on my company's website: www.keatsconnelly.com/preferred-currency-exchange.

4. Hiring a Property Manager

If you become the owner of one or more rental homes that is located thousands of miles away, you should definitely consider hiring a local property manager. You can start interviewing potential managers by asking for referrals from your real estate agent. Here are some questions to ask potential property managers:

1. Are you paying the real estate agent a fee or commission if I use your services? (Consider: How objective was your agent in making this referral?)

2. How long have you been a property manager and can you provide me with referrals?

3. How many properties do you manage?

4. How many Canadian owners do you manage properties for?

5. What staff do you have? Do you do all of this yourself or do you have employees or do you outsource some of the work?

6. Can I have sample agreements to review, such as a rental agreement and the agreement between property owner and property manager?

7. How are your fees calculated and are they guaranteed for a period of time?

8. Are there other fees such as a "vacancy fee," "set-up fee," "leasing fee," etc.?

9. Would I be locked into this agreement for some period of time, or can I leave at any time?

10. Would you be providing me copies of all receipts and a full accounting monthly?

4.1 Tenant rights laws

One very important reason to hire a professional property manager is that he or she will know what rights tenants have in the state in which you have your property. Nolo has a site that gives an overview of the landlord-tenant laws in each state: www.nolo.com/legal-encyclopedia/state-landlord-tenant-laws. Even if you manage properties at home, I suggest that you do not try to manage your US properties, because not only are the laws different between the US and Canada, but laws vary from state to state.

Some of the areas that you or the property manager will need to know and tread carefully in are:

• Required landlord disclosures

• Security deposit limits and deadlines

• Late fees

• Tenant's right to withhold rent

- Termination and eviction

- Landlord rights to access of rental property

If you insist on managing your US properties yourself, at least seek the counsel of a good landlord-tenant attorney. Note, that this attorney will most likely not be the same attorney you used to form your entity or from whom you received tax advice.

5. Alberta Reciprocal Enforcement of Judgments Act and Other Reciprocal Laws

The *Alberta Reciprocal Enforcement of Judgments Act* allows enforcement of a judgment from one jurisdiction within Canada to another, and with many states in the US.

In 1962 the Uniform Foreign Money Judgments Recognition Act was passed in the US to enforce the judgments between states under the Full Faith and Credit clause of the US Constitution. To meet the increased needs for enforcement of foreign country money-judgments, the Uniform Foreign-Country Money Judgments Recognition Act was placed into law in 2005.

If the US and the states wanted their foreign judgments to be honored, they would have to enter into reciprocal agreements with other countries and as of 2016, the following states have enacted reciprocal laws; Arizona, Washington, Oregon, California, Nevada, Idaho, Montana, Colorado, New Mexico, Oklahoma, Minnesota, Iowa, Illinois, Indiana, Michigan, Alabama, Georgia, Virginia, North Carolina, Delaware, Hawaii, and the District of Columbia. During 2016, New Jersey and Massachusetts introduced bills that will allow reciprocal judgments.

What this means is that if you default on a loan in one of the reciprocal states, say Arizona, the creditor can file a judgment in Canada and it will be enforced, and vice versa. In short this means that you should consider taking steps to protect your Canadian assets. This was discussed in some detail in Chapter 2.

Conclusion

For a Canadian, buying real estate in the United States is relatively easy, so much so that many investors have a false sense of security. There are many things to consider and numerous ways in which things can go wrong. My sincere hope is that I have made the topic a little less confusing.

My goal has been to educate you on the major issues that confront nearly every Canadian investor in US real estate. I briefly explain the opportunity, the buying process, talk about US mortgages, direct and indirect ownership methods, income tax, estate tax, probate, and other things you should know. This book attempts to answer the major questions Canadian investors and their advisers have about buying real estate in the US; those questions include:

- How should I own the property?

- What are the tax consequences and how do I minimize my tax liability?

- How do I report the income on my tax returns?

- Am I subject to US estate tax, and if so, how do I avoid it?

- How do I avoid or reduce my personal liability from lawsuits if I an renting my property?

- What are my tax filing requirements?

I have incorporated both technical and practical issues and explanations, giving helpful hints, cautions, and examples.

Although I have done my best to take a complex set of laws and explain them in some detail, I do not suggest that you attempt to do it yourself. There is an important distinction between knowledge and wisdom. Wisdom is defined as the ability to make sensible decisions and judgments based on personal knowledge and experience. I have attempted to impart knowledge, but knowledge without experience frequently turns to folly.

When I was younger and had more time, I loved to play chess. I read many books written by chess grandmasters on the subject. Even though I have read the books (knowledge) and played the games (experience), I have never been able to call myself an expert at chess. Just like my chess analogy, you cannot expect to read a book and perform at the level necessary for success. You need an experienced professional to make sense of and to provide advice on the nuances of each situation.

Please seek out knowledgeable and experienced professionals when needed — your return on investment may well exceed that of the real estate you are buying.

I wish you success in all of your investments!

Appendix I: Checklist for Buying Real Estate in the US

Educate yourself about what is involved with owning real estate in another country, such as the following:

- ☐ Income taxes (how much, when, and how paid)?

- ☐ Nonresident estate taxes (Will they apply to you? If so, find out how to avoid.)

- ☐ Decide how best to own the property (see Chapter 2).

- ☐ Learn what sort of non-tax reporting is required by Canada and the US.

- ☐ Locate an experienced cross-border tax professional.

- ☐ If necessary, have an attorney establish the proper US business entity to hold the property.

- ☐ Obtain Employer Identification Number (EIN) and/or Individual Taxpayer Identification Number (ITIN), as appropriate.

- [ ] Locate an experienced realtor who has experience working with Canadians.

- [ ] If needed, identify lending sources.

- [ ] If renting, locate a property manager experienced with foreign buyers.

- [ ] Purchase real estate.

- [ ] If property is being rented, submit Certificate of Foreign Person's Claim That Income Is Effectively Connected with the Conduct of a Trade or Business in the United States (Form W-8ECI) to the property manager or tenant.

- [ ] Complete withholding forms: Annual Return for Partnership Withholding Tax (Form 8804), Foreign Partner's Information Statement of Section 1446 Withholding Tax (Form 8805), and Partnership Withholding Tax Payment Voucher (Form 8813), as necessary.

- [ ] If a US entity was used to purchase the property, the entity must file a tax return by March 15 for corporations and April 15 for partnerships. A revocable living trust is not required to file a tax return; all income is reported on your individual tax return.

- [ ] If the property was rented, in nearly all cases, you will need to file US Nonresident Alien Income Tax Return (Form 1040NR) by June 15 of each year.

- [ ] File Bureau of Economic Analysis Survey of Foreign Direct Investment in the US (Form BE-15) by May 31 or by February 15 for Transactions of US Affiliate, Except a US Banking Affiliate, with Foreign Parent (BE-605), if required.

- [ ] When selling a property that exceeds $300,000, look into the necessity of filing Application for Withholding Certificate for Dispositions by Foreign Persons of the US Real Property Interests (Form 8288-B) to reduce the withholding tax.

Appendix II: Resources

Cross-Border Tax Help

- KeatsConnelly: www.keatsconnelly.com

- Cross Border Tax & Accounting: www.cbta.net

- Cross-Border Books: www.crossborderbooks.net

- Self-Counsel Press Cross-Border Series:
  www.self-counsel.com/personal-finance/cross-border.html

US Tax Resources

- Internal Revenue Service (IRS): www.irs.gov

- Foreign Investment in Real Property Tax Act Withholding:
  www.irs.gov/individuals/international-taxpayers/
  firpta-withholding

- IRS Forms and Publications:
  https://www.irs.gov/forms-pubs

IRS Forms

- 1040NR (Individual Tax Return for Nonresident Alien):
  www.irs.gov/pub/irs-pdf/f1040nr.pdf

- 1065 (US Partnership Return):
  www.irs.gov/pub/irs-pdf/f1065.pdf

- 1120 (US Corporation Tax Return):
  www.irs.gov/pub/irs-pdf/f1120.pdf

- 1120-F (Corporate Tax Return for a Foreign Corporation):
  www.irs.gov/pub/irs-pdf/f1120f.pdf

- W-7 (Application for IRS ID Number):
  www.irs.gov/pub/irs-pdf/fw7.pdf

- 706-NA (United States Estate [and Generation-Skipping Transfer] Tax Return):
  www.irs.gov/pub/irs-pdf/f706na.pdf

- W-8ECI (Certificate of Foreign Person's Claim That Income Is Effectively Connected to US Trade or Business):
  www.irs.gov/pub/irs-pdf/fw8eci.pdf

- W-9 (Request for Taxpayer Identification Number and Certification):
  www.irs.gov/pub/irs-pdf/fw9.pdf

- 8288 (US Withholding Tax Return for Dispositions by Foreign Persons of US Real Property Interests):
  www.irs.gov/pub/irs-pdf/f8288.pdf

- 8288-B (Application for Withholding Certificate for Dispositions by Foreign Persons of US Real Property Interests):
  www.irs.gov/pub/irs-pdf/f8288b.pdf

IRS Publications

- Publication 515 – Withholding of Tax on Nonresident Aliens and Foreign Entities:
  www.irs.gov/pub/irs-pdf/p515.pdf

- Publication 597 – Information on the United States-Canada Income Tax Treaty:
  www.irs.gov/pub/irs-pdf/p597.pdf

- Publication 527 – Residential Rental Property:
  www.irs.gov/pub/irs-pdf/p527.pdf

- Tax Foundation: www.taxfoundation.org

- Tax Policy Center: http://taxpolicycenter.org/

- Tax-Rates.org:
  www.tax-rates.org/taxtables/corporate-income-tax-by-state

State Tax Sites

- California Franchise Tax Board: www.ftb.ca.gov

- Arizona Department of Revenue: www.azdor.gov

- Hawaii Department of Revenue: www.tax.hawaii.gov

- Nevada Department of Revenue: www.tax.nv.gov

- Texas Comptroller of Public Accounts:
  www.comptroller.texas.gov/taxes

- Florida Department of Revenue:
  http://dor.myflorida.com/taxes/Pages/default.aspx

Canadian Tax Resources

- Canada Revenue Agency (CRA):
  www.cra-arc.gc.ca

Canadian Forms

- Form T1135 (Foreign Income Verification Statement):
  www.cra-arc.gc.ca/E/pbg/tf/t1135/t1135-14e.pdf

- Form T1134 (Information Return Relating to Controlled and Not-Controlled Foreign Affiliates):
  www.cra-arc.gc.ca/E/pbg/tf/t1134/t1134-12e.pdf

For Renters

- Registration of Arizona Residential Rental Property: www.azdor.gov/Portals/0/Forms/82901.pdf

- All Property Management: www.allpropertymanagement.com

Other Resources

- Bureau of Economic Analysis (BEA): www.bea.gov

- BE-10 (Benchmark Survey of US Direct Investment Abroad: www.bea.gov/surveys/respondent_be10.htm

- BE-15 (Survey of Foreign Direct Investment in the US): http://bea.gov/surveys/pdf/be15claim_web.pdf

- Closing costs maps: http://bankrate.com

- National Buyer's Agent Alliance: http://buyersagent.net

Realtor Associations

- National Association of Realtors: www.realtor.org

- Arizona Association of Realtors: http://aaronline.com

- California Association of Realtors: www.car.org

- Florida Association of Realtors: www.floridarealtors.org

- Nevada Association of Realtors: www.nvar.org

- Realtor.com: www.realtor.com

- Homes.com: www.homes.com

- MLS.com: www.mls.com

About the Author

Since he was young, Dale Walters has had a passion for helping others. He considered both the traditionally helpful fields of law and medicine, but his natural talent for numbers led him into accounting, an industry that helps people with some of the hardest decisions in their lives: financial decisions.

He has been helping people with their financial decisions since 1980. Along the way, Walters earned both the US Certified Financial Planner™ (CFP®) and Certified Public Accountant designations, and even spent time in the tax department of the "Big Four" accounting firm of KPMG.

Walters' life has been a series of fortunate events. Working at KPMG was no different. While there, he got involved with preparing international tax returns of foreign individuals working in the Phoenix offices of Motorola. After a few years with KPMG, Walters went to work for a small CPA firm in Scottsdale, Arizona. This led him to a fateful meeting with Bob Keats and Tom Connelly, founders of KeatsConnelly in early 1994 and within six months, he joined the team, and in 1999 became a shareholder.

In keeping with the fortunate events in his life, working at KeatsConnelly afforded Walters a mentor in Bob Keats. In addition to being a dual citizen of the United States and Canada, and one of the top cross-border advisors, Keats is also the author of *The Border Guide*, and *A Canadian's Best Tax Haven: The US*. Armed with his mentor, Walters earned his Canadian CFP® designation, making him one of the very first people to hold designations on both sides of the border. By 2004, he was named the CEO of the firm.

Since joining the leadership team of KeatsConnelly, Walters has helped the firm earn awards for ethics, community volunteerism, workplace flexibility, company culture, and a Community Impact award for being one of the top businesses in Arizona. All of this has led KeatsConnelly to being one of Arizona's most admired companies.

Dale is an author and frequent speaker, and has been quoted in *The Globe and Mail, National Post, USA Today, Los Angeles Times, Chicago Tribune, Wall Street Journal,* and *Arizona Republic*, to name a few. In addition to writing this book, Dale is the co-author of *Taxation of Canadians in America*, and *Taxation of Americans in Canada*.

On the personal side, Walters has a passion for both wrestling and martial arts. Both passions have served him well. Wrestling helped him to earn him a college scholarship back in the 1970s, which led to meeting his wife of three decades, which led him to being a dad of two wonderful children. Martial arts helped him achieve inner peace as well as World Heavyweight Karate championships from 1986 to 1989.

Both on a personal level and as part of a company, his greatest rewards continue to come from helping people. That is ultimately why he wrote this book; to help you avoid the many potential mistakes that can be made when buying real estate in the United States.